BEATING BURNOUT
in Youth Ministry

Dean Feldmeyer

BEATING BURNOUT
in Youth Ministry

Loveland, Colorado

Beating Burnout in Youth Ministry

Designed by Judy Bienick

ISBN 0-931529-47-6
Printed in the United States of America

For Jean, Ben and Sarah
. . . and the rest of my family

Contents

Taking Care of Your Ministry

Taking Care of Yourself

Flirting With Burnout

I've been doing youth ministry for a long time. I deal with the same frustrations, anxieties, problems and concerns as everyone else in youth ministry. Through it all, I've been fairly successful at juggling my ministry, writing, family, speaking engagements and other interests.

But I do get in trouble from time to time. Occasionally I find myself about to go under, weighed down by too many commitments and not enough time.

Like many other youth workers, I flirt with burnout.

But I haven't let burnout take me under. Somehow I've managed to work through the frustrations, overcome the anxieties, solve the problems and deal with the concerns. I'm still doing youth ministry long after others my age and with my experience have moved on to other vocations and ministries.

It occurred to me that I must have found something to keep me in youth ministry. It isn't the big bucks, and it isn't the short, regular hours. It isn't the 60-hour workweek or the small office or the carwashes. I must have discovered something that makes it all work for me.

So I began writing this book with the goal of discovering what I knew about youth ministry that made it so easy and rewarding for me. I wanted to share what I discovered with you, hoping it would help you.

Here's what I discovered as I examined my career: The key is *time management*. Through all these years, I've learned to manage my time—work time, family time, recreational time, personal time—in a way that's kept me from burning out and getting out long ago. My question has always been, "How can I manage my work demands so they don't overwhelm me and leave me with nothing for the other parts of my life?"

Besides not burning out, I've been able to enjoy my job, spend time with my family, find opportunities to speak and write, and relish the possibility of becoming an old-timer of my field by the time I'm 40.

A Modest Proposal

I hope you'll read this book three times. (I know what you're thinking: "If I had time to read it three times, I wouldn't need to read it." But hear me out.)

First, just skim the chapters, reading only the stuff that jumps off the page and makes you say, "That's me!" Then put the book aside for a couple of days, and let those thoughts simmer.

The second time, read it with a pencil in your hand. Read the chapters that really demand to be read. Underline, answer questions and fill in the blanks. If you find a suggestion that sounds really good, use it. It's yours. Then put the book aside and spend some time implementing the ideas you picked up.

Now, after you've tried a couple of changes, read the rest of the book. Or, better yet, read the whole thing cover to cover. Take what you need and use it.

Then put the book on a shelf. But remember the categories and chapter headings. Keep it within reach. If you feel things getting out of hand in some area, grab the book and read the relevant chapter again. (This especially applies to the chapter on "How to Say No." If you are a "yes" person you'll probably have to read this chapter at least once a year for the rest of your life. I do.)

However you choose to read the book, have fun with it. I had fun writing it. And if you see a little of yourself in it, take heart. You're not alone. I couldn't have written it without seeing something of myself in each chapter.

CHAPTER 1

Where Does the Time Go?

E ver feel guilty about brushing your teeth? I don't. As I
squirt that little blob of toothpaste onto my brush, I
don't hear my conscience saying, "Well, aren't we selfish
taking time for ourself?"

After all, brushing my teeth is just something I do. I
learned early in life that dental hygiene is important. So I
take the time each day to tend to it.

There's nothing wrong with taking care of ourselves. We
do it all the time in a hundred different ways. We bathe. We
wash our clothes. We brush our teeth. We may even floss.

Many people carry this same principle into the work
place. For example, carpenters never feel guilty about sharpening their saws. Their job depends upon well-maintained
saws, hammers, levels and squares. They insist on taking
care of their tools. No apologies. No excuses. No guilt.

But lots of youth ministers manage to forget their own
needs. It used to happen to me somewhere between hanging up the toothbrush and arriving at work. I'd get so
wrapped up in what I was doing that I'd forget to take care
of my tools—my energy, creativity, time and commitment.

Worse yet, I used to feel guilty when I took any time
for myself. Something inside said I was being selfish. I
wasn't giving the "hunert- 'n' -ten percent" it took to do the
job right. After all, there were so many demands, distrac-

tions and downright crises in youth ministry.

A couple of years ago, my daily schedule looked something like this:

6:30 a.m. Get up, shower, get dressed, start breakfast.

7:00 a.m. Wake up kids. Put clothes in washer.

7:10 a.m. Make sure kids are up.

7:30 a.m. Serve breakfast. Pack lunches.

8:00 a.m. Get kids off to school, put clothes in dryer, clean up breakfast mess. Kiss wife goodbye.

9:00 a.m. Arrive at church. Check messages. Chitchat with secretary.

9:15 a.m. Plan agenda for meeting tonight. Make copies.

10:00 a.m. Staff meeting.

11:15 a.m. Work on newsletter. Interrupted by phone calls and office visits.

12:15 p.m. Luncheon with other youth ministers.

1:30 p.m. Work on newsletter. More interruptions.

2:45 p.m. Check mail and answer letters. More phone calls to return (left over from morning).

3:00 p.m. Plan for youth group meeting.

3:30 p.m. Run errands: Pick up stuff needed for youth group meeting. Stop at dry cleaners and grocery store. Mail letters.

4:30 p.m. Home. Jog.

5:00 p.m. Dinner with family.

6:00 p.m. Help kids with homework.

7:00 p.m. Meeting at church.

9:00 p.m. Back home. Try to return phone calls one more time.

10:00 p.m. Help wife sort laundry from this morning. Set table for breakfast.

10:45 p.m. Sit down and read newspaper. Watch TV news. Fall asleep in chair.

11:30 p.m. Go to bed.

Does this schedule look anything like yours? You can run a routine like this for a while—maybe even for years. But I've got news: Eventually you're going to burn out. (There, I said it—the "b" word.)

That's what nearly happened to me. I had no time for

recreation. There was no time for recharging my batteries. And God help me if the car broke down or I needed to go to the dentist or one of my children got sick. I was a busy, busy person. My sense of obligation, commitment and self-sacrifice was running me into the ground.

How did I beat burnout? I realized that ministry is long-term work, more like a marathon than a sprint. My tools for ministry require maintenance. And the most important tool I have is myself. Unless I take care of myself, I'm in no position to take care of others.

Our Basic Needs

Every human being must satisfy some basic needs. Those of us in ministry (volunteer or professional) are no exception. The basic needs include:

- shelter and food;
- personal space;
- a sense of belonging;
- love (both given and received);
- rest, relaxation and recreation; and
- the chance to create or build.

I usually hear one of three reactions to this list. Some say: "Hey, no problem. I take care of all that stuff. My needs are being met just fine."

Others say: "Yes, I know. I really do need these things. But who has the time? There just aren't enough hours in the day. I guess I'll just learn to live without them."

Finally, there are those who say: "I know! I want all these things. But no one cuts me any slack. People won't let me take the time."

I want to react to these responses. In fact, I think addressing them is the key to beating burnout. Let me start with the first.

Being Honest About Your Needs

I hear the first response most often from people in professional ministry. Their needs are being met, they say. Then the next minute they tell me about inadequate par-

sonages and broken-down cars. They eat meals on the run
at fast-food joints. They miss their child's Little League
games. And they go weeks (sometimes months) on end
without a day off.

Something is wrong with this picture.

Try the "Where Have All the Hours Gone?" exercise to
assess how your needs are being met.

If you have more than 168 hours in column A, you've
overestimated some of your activities (there are only 168
hours in a week). Take another look. Do you *really* spend
that much time on relationships? rest and relaxation? spiritual life?

More important, look at the total in column B. If you're
like most youth ministers, it's probably much higher than
168. Most of us want to spend more time on non-work activities because those activities meet some of our basic
needs. But we don't take the time.

Ask some serious questions about your current schedule. Do you feel hurried and hassled? Or do you feel con-
tent and fulfilled? Is anything missing from your current
schedule?

Is your life balanced? Is it moving toward goals or just
scrambling to put out fires? Do you tend to all your needs?
Is something being left out altogether?

Unmet basic needs—even as basic as shelter and transportation—can halt your ability to serve. Can you make
hospital calls effectively when you're worried about your
car getting there and back? Can you concentrate on tonight's meeting when your roof is leaking and ruining your
carpet?

Look through the list of basic needs on page 13 one
more time. Ask yourself if they are met—*adequately*. Are
you free and energized to do the ministry you want? Or are
unmet needs holding you back?

In tending to our basic needs, we all probably have
room for improvement. But there just isn't enough time!

Finding the Time

All of us have those days when there simply isn't

Where Have All the Hours Gone?

Instructions: In column A, estimate how many hours you spend each week in each of the following areas of life (be honest!). Next, write in column B how much time you'd *like* to spend in each area of life. What would your ideal week look like?

When you're finished, write the total number of hours for each column.

	A	B
• Work—Working in all facets, at home or at the office (even the fun stuff).	_____	_____
• Sleep—Sleeping at night and in naps.	_____	_____
• Relationships—Building relationships with family, spouse, friends, extended family.	_____	_____
• Home—Working around the house doing chores, fixing things, doing laundry, working in the yard, fixing the car, working on taxes.	_____	_____
• Spiritual life—Praying, studying the Bible, meditating.	_____	_____
• Health—Eating, exercising, mental health, dental health, physical health.	_____	_____
• Recreation—Doing hobbies and any other recreational activities.	_____	_____
• Rest and relaxation—Consuming junk food for the brain and body such as watching the tube or recreational reading.	_____	_____
• Continuing education—Sharpening your skills.	_____	_____
• Miscellaneous—Waiting in line, daydreaming.	_____	_____
• **Totals**	_____	_____

enough time to get everything else done and still take care of ourselves. (For some youth ministers, every day is like that.) We simply can't find the time. Which brings us to the second response: "There just aren't enough hours in a day."

Perhaps the problem is that we keep looking for more time. I think I used to expect to find "the time"—as though it were out there waiting to be found. I used to have time when I was a kid. Maybe I misplaced it.

Time isn't like your keys or gloves. It doesn't lie around until you stumble over it so you can use it again. If you're going to take your own needs seriously, you have to *make* time.

This book is filled with practical ways to make time. That's what time management is all about: sharpening your schedule so that it leaves time for self-care.

To be honest, though, I really don't like the term "time management." It sounds like I've got this huge mass of time I must figure out how to manage. The exact opposite is really true for most of us because we have so little time.

There's an old superstition in professional baseball that a bat has only a certain number of hits in it. If you let someone else use your bat and he gets a hit, that's one less hit for you from that bat. So superstitious professional baseball players carefully guard their bats.

I wonder if we shouldn't approach our lives and ministries that way. We each only have so many heartbeats in our life. Only a certain number of minutes, a certain number of hours. We have only so many Sunday evenings and Saturday afternoons.

Consider that you may only have 75 summers in your life. How many have you already spent? How many do you have left? How will you spend the next one?

There's so much to do and so little time. When you look at life that way, the issue is not really "time management" but "activity management." If you can learn to manage your work activities more effectively, you'll have more time for your non-work activities. That's what this book is about.

Taking Charge

The third response ("Nobody cuts me any slack") is the saddest one of the three. People who respond in this way know they have basic needs. They may even know how to make time for them. But they're waiting for permission to take care of themselves.

It'd be great to hear: "Gosh, you look tired. Why don't you take a day off?" or "Gee, what a terrible old car you have. Here's a raise to buy yourself a new one."

But chances are good that no one will say those things to you. Only you know your needs. Only you know what it will take to meet those needs. You have to make the decisions and take action for yourself.

It's up to you. Don't wait for permission to take care of yourself. Start making time for yourself. Learn to work quickly and efficiently. Then take the time you've created to live a more balanced life. Do it for yourself, your ministry and those you love.

CHAPTER 2

The Big Picture

...

Taking Care of Your Ministry

■ CHAPTER 2 ■

The Big Picture

Recently a friend confessed to me her discontent with her youth ministry. Kathy had been at the same church for four years, and her once vibrant program was dwindling. Fewer kids showed up. Those who attended seemed bored with the activities. Kathy was tired of creating programs that flopped. She was tired of struggling to get the kids involved. And if one more adult volunteer were to resign, Kathy thought she might resign too.

Kathy was burned out.

It only took a few questions to discover Kathy's problem. You see, Kathy ran the same program this year that she put together when she started. Sure, she'd made some minor modifications. But the program wasn't keeping pace with all the changes in Kathy's group—or in Kathy.

Kathy's church is located in a growing suburban area. During the past four years, two new developments were completed, and a major shopping mall opened. With the influx of new, young families, many more youth group members babysit regularly. Other group members have part-time jobs at the mall. And many of the kids prefer the new community center to the church's open gym nights.

Two years ago, Kathy got married. Her lifestyle changed considerably. She and her husband want to start a family, but Kathy worries about juggling the youth ministry with motherhood. Actually, motherhood seems like the perfect reason to tender her resignation.

The bottom line: Kathy is wasting her and her group's

time with an obsolete program. By reassessing her own strengths and weaknesses and the needs of the young people in her church, Kathy can design a program that once again meets her own needs and the needs of her youth ministry. The result will be new enthusiasm, not only among group members but also in Kathy.

Taking Inventory

Whether I'm in a new position or an old one, or whether I'm starting from scratch or taking over an established program, I like to stop and take inventory once in a while.

I have a quick, reliable method I use every couple of years to reassess my situation. I look at myself as a youth worker. Then I look at the kids in my community. Armed with this information, I develop or modify the youth ministry goals—for myself and the group. Here are the tools I use. Use them as they are, or adjust them to fit your own needs and preferences.

Who Am I?

I start by taking a test—half in fun, half serious—to check out where I am as a youth worker. I call it the "Youth Leader's Personality and Style Inventory."

Try it. Answer the following questions as truthfully as possible. (There are, of course, no right or wrong answers.)

Youth Leader's Personality and Style Inventory

My name is _____

My nickname is _____

If I had an Indian name it would be _____

Ten things I like:

1. _____   6. _____
2. _____   7. _____
3. _____   8. _____
4. _____   9. _____
5. _____   10. _____

Ten things I could live without:

1. _____   6. _____
2. _____   7. _____
3. _____   8. _____
4. _____   9. _____
5. _____   10. _____

My favorite food is

_____

My favorite place is

_____

My car is a

_____

If I had a choice, my car would be a

_____

Three things I'm really good at:

1. _____
2. _____
3. _____

Three things I'm not so good at:

1. _____
2. _____
3. _____

The thing I'm best at is

_____

The thing I'm worst at is

_____

If I could be a character in a famous book, I would be _____

_____

My favorite scripture passage is _____

The biblical character I most identify with is _____

_____

I'm a youth worker because

_____

_____

The biggest frustration of youth work is

_____

_____

The greatest reward of youth work is

_____

If I had more time I'd

_____

_____

If I had $100 I'd

_____

_____

If I had $1 I'd

_____

_____

If I couldn't do my current job, I'd _____

_____

Sometimes I wonder if the church will ever

_____

_____

I was most proud of my church when

_____

_____

Five years from now I'll be

_____

_____

Ten years from now I'll be

_____

_____

Twenty years from now I'll be

_____

_____

I intend to do youth ministry until

_____

_____

I'd like to see this youth ministry

_____

_____

One way I can help achieve this goal is to

_____

_____

Okay, you may put down your pencil. You've completed the inventory's personality phase. When you feel adequately rested, proceed to the inventory's style phase. For each statement, checkmark the box that best describes you.

1. When I see the need for a change I usually act
   ☐ yesterday.
   ☐ immediately.
   ☐ within a couple of days.
   ☐ when I get around to it.
   ☐ Trying to change things only gets me into trouble.
2. When I want something I don't have, I usually
   ☐ go after it, no matter what the cost.
   ☐ work out a reasonable plan to get it.
   ☐ see if I can get someone to get it for me.
   ☐ complain.
3. When I play volleyball, I usually
   ☐ take no prisoners.
   ☐ spike that sucker down their throats.
   ☐ make sure everyone rotates correctly.
   ☐ keep score from the sidelines.
   ☐ tend to be injured.
4. When pizza is served, I usually
   ☐ dive headfirst for those big pieces.
   ☐ count the pieces and announce to everyone what his or her share is.
   ☐ make sure the kids get some, and take a piece for myself if there's any left.
   ☐ squirrel some away for myself, for later.
   ☐ don't like pizza.
5. When a group member gets hurt, I usually
   ☐ tell the teenager that pain builds character and that he or she should try to "play through" the pain.
   ☐ put an ice pack on it and look at it later.
   ☐ give the teenager chicken soup and a hug.
   ☐ administer fast and efficient first aid.
   ☐ rush the injured person to the nearest emergency room.
6. When the pastor disagrees with something I want to do, I usually
   ☐ punch out the pastor.
   ☐ threaten to resign.
   ☐ do what I want to do, but call it something else.
   ☐ fold to the pastor's wishes.
   ☐ decline talking to the pastor.

7. When the church bus breaks down on a long trip, I
   ☐ curse at it and kick the tires.
   ☐ sit down on the curb and cry.
   ☐ fix it myself, no matter how long it takes.
   ☐ call a mechanic.
   ☐ quit using church buses.
8. When picking a movie for my youth group, I usually
   ☐ find anything the kids will come see, preferably something rated R and full of violence.
   ☐ find something that's relevant and rated G or PG.
   ☐ play it safe and stick with Disney movies.
   ☐ play it really safe and stick with "religious" films.
   ☐ decline—it's a no-win situation.
9. When there's a troublemaker in the group, I usually
   ☐ slap the kid around a little.
   ☐ threaten to tell his or her parents.
   ☐ throw the kid out of the group.
   ☐ pray for the young person.
   ☐ say that there's no such thing as a bad kid—only inept sponsors.
10. When recruiting youth sponsors, I usually go after
    ☐ big, scary guys with bad breath.
    ☐ attractive members of the opposite sex.
    ☐ someone who will agree with me no matter what I say.
    ☐ someone with some skills and energy.
    ☐ any warm body.
    ☐ Youth sponsor? What's that?

Congratulations! You've completed the inventory. It wasn't that hard, was it? Now comes the fun part.

Go back over the inventory and pretend you don't know the person who answered the questions. Ask yourself some questions about this person:

● What kind of person do I have here? What are some adjectives I'd use to describe this person? Shy? Self-confident? Brave? Brash? Resourceful? Honest? Single-minded?

● What special gifts does this person have to offer teen-agers? What strengths can he or she rely on? What weaknesses should he or she work on?

● Does this person act out of his or her gut, heart or head? Is he or she task-, process-, goal- or maintenance-oriented?

● How can this person be used for God's kingdom?

● How can this person's style and personality be understood as a gift of the Holy Spirit?

● How is God reflected in this person's style?

● How can this person's personality lead young people to a more profound faith?

Caricatures of Youth Workers

Want to try another exercise? "Do You Recognize Yourself?" (page 28) shows 15 caricatures of youth workers. Look through the list. Which one best describes you? (If none of these caricatures fits you, maybe you're a hybrid. Make up another caricature that fits you better.)

In what ways does the caricature fit you? Share your perceptions with your family or a support group. How do you feel about it? Write a few lines in your personal journal. Ask about your caricature the same questions that were asked after the "Youth Leader's Personality and Style Inventory."

Why did we do all these exercises? Because we have to know ourselves as youth workers—our strengths, weaknesses, gifts, graces and personality traits. And we all have to get reacquainted with ourselves once in a while. We all change. We learn new things, get new ideas, grow tired of old methods and expand our horizons.

Remember Kathy? She's still the same person. But her interests and abilities have changed. She's still involved in ministry, but as a married woman she spends more of her time and energy on family issues. She has less time for herself and will have even less as a mother. But her husband enjoys doing things with the youth group, so she has a new resource in him.

By taking the time to look at herself, Kathy can get ideas for potential changes in her youth ministry. In other words, Kathy needs to get a good handle on who she is as a youth worker.

So do I. So do you. By the way, it's fun to look back at old inventories and see how you've changed. It's also important to your ministry. It reminds you where you've been and where you're going—and growing.

Who Are My Kids?

In the same way we need to examine *ourselves* to stay fresh, we need to be sure we know the *kids* we minister to. Otherwise, our programs risk meeting needs that aren't there. The result is personal frustration, which drains our energy and vision for ministry.

Recently I overheard a conversation between two pastors. It went something like this:

"Hey, Tom. How goes it in the new church? Beginning to get the lay of the land?"

"Still kind of feeling my way along, Harry. I'm concentrating on meeting folks, you know? I want to call on everyone in the congregation at least once during these first 18 months or so."

"Woah! That's a lot of calling. Don't you do anything else?"

"Sure. Some stuff's got to be done. But I figure the first priority is getting to know folks, you know? Meet them where they are. Find out what makes them tick."

"I hear you. Programs are fine, but in a new church you've got to put first things first. Be a good pastor and programs will take care of themselves, I always say."

"Always say that, do you?"

"Well, sometimes I say it."

"You just made it up, just now."

"Yeah. But I wish I always said it."

And off these two pastors go to have a cup of coffee and take their ministries slow and easy. They're careful. They tread softly. They take time getting to know each and every church member. Then and only then do they worry about programs. Year by year they each build their lives and ministries into a well-established institution.

It would be nice if we youth ministers could do that.

Do You Recognize Yourself?

The Drill Sergeant. Gets things done. Can organize a carwash in 10 seconds flat. Barks orders and is obeyed. Always has a plan. Feelings are for sissies.

The Earth Mother. Always on hand with a batch of homemade cookies. Great in the kitchen and has lots of home remedies, especially hugs and sympathies for whatever ails you. Not much of a leader, but a great support person.

The Coach. Lots of pep talks. Makes you proud to be part of the team. Prefers to keep score rather than play games. Does well when in charge, but tends to chafe under another person's leadership.

The Cheerleader. Our little spark plug. Always has a positive word for everyone. Cheerful. Peppy. Bouncy. Sometimes has a hard time being serious.

The Perpetual Teenager. Wants to be "one of the kids." Knows all the Top 40 songs by heart. Knows all the popular jargon—and uses it. Couldn't be firm with the group if life depended on it.

The Pastor. Leads meaningful worship services and prays beautiful prayers. Talks religion like a pro. Couldn't hit a softball if it were as big as a house.

The Ex-Doper. Has seen it all and probably done it all. Is shocked by nothing, surprised by nothing. Laid back and a little cynical. Or "born again" and talks endlessly about how rotten he or she was in the past.

The Prophet. Deeply into social issues: hunger, whales, pollution, abortion . . . whatever's hot. Has trouble having a good time. Favorite phrase: "Nobody cares anymore."

The Comedian. Really popular with the kids. Funny. Has a pun for every situation. Makes fun of self. Has a favorite stand-up comic, and knows all his or her routines by heart.

The Politician. Great recruiter. Will tell anybody anything to get them to the youth group meetings. Makes lots of promises but never really commits to them. Looks great!

 The Toastmaster. Works well in front of the group. Has good stories, speeches, lessons and audio-visuals. Feels uncomfortable in one-to-one situations. Hates small talk.

The Jock. Has memorized all the game books and can play every game better than anyone in the youth group. Plays for blood and wouldn't think of changing the rules to favor the underdog. Wears nothing but sweats or jogging shorts.

 The Professor. Knows something about everything. Can usually fix things that are broken—or at least tells you why they aren't working. Smokes a pipe. Has lots of theories about youth work. Will probably try them out sometime.

The Folk Singer. Usually plays a guitar. Can lead singing but really prefers to perform for the group. Knows every song John Denver ever recorded. Has never heard of Petra.

 The Dad or Mom. Genuinely likes kids but doesn't really know what to do or say around them. Thinks they are cute or funny. Usually will drive or cook or do any number of support functions but doesn't want to be in the limelight.

The Hybrid. (Describe yourself here.) _____

_____

_____

_____

Unfortunately, we don't have time.

Pastors usually have a little more luxury with time than youth ministers. Not only do they tend to stay at a church longer, but their congregations consist mostly of adults. Some people will move away and others will come in. But, basically, most congregations are relatively stable.

Youth ministry, on the other hand, is highly unstable. Senior high youth groups completely change every four years. So if I spend the next year and a half visiting every young person in the church and/or community, the seniors will have graduated and a whole new class of freshmen will have come in before I finish. The visiting would never end.

Also, I can't let programs wait until I've finished meeting my congregation. While I firmly believe that real ministry takes place in relationships, I also know those relationships usually form in the context of programs. Yet I can't expect to create meaningful programs if I don't know the people I'm supposed to minister to. If I'm not careful, I can spend lots of time and energy creating programs that *simply* fail. Like Kathy, I may start feeling lousy, desperate and burned out.

To keep from missing the mark, I periodically ask the same kinds of questions about the young people I serve as I ask about myself.

Who are they?

What are their needs? How do they perceive their needs?

What are they interested in?

What do they do in their spare time if they have any?

How do they spend their money? energy? time?

What concerns do they have? What kinds of relationships do they have with teachers, parents, peers and neighbors?

Unfortunately, I can't visit every single kid to answer these questions. I don't have time. But I can set the big picture—a broad, general idea of who the kids are and what they need. Impressions and generalizations aren't always completely accurate. But in the absence of specific data, they can be helpful.

Here are some quick ways to get that big picture. Why not try them in your own youth ministry?

● **Maps**—Drive through the community. When you

complete the drive, draw a map, similar to the "Sample Map." (Use the "Map of (your community)" to draw your own map. The symbol in the middle represents your church. Include the community's highlights and important landmarks. Then ask yourself: Why are these important? How has the community identified them? Does the community seem to have some natural dividers, areas of concentration or types of areas?

Now compare your rough map with an actual map of the community. How do they compare? What impressions do the similarities and differences give you of the area?

On the actual map, mark the homes of active youth group members. How are they distributed throughout the community? What does that distribution tell you about the kids and their needs?

● **Phone directories**—These often contain information about the community's history, current population, churches, schools and so on. That's useful background information for understanding where kids come from and where they live.

● **Real estate offices**—Visit a local real estate office and ask for printed information on the community. Real estate agents are usually delighted to share information about the community's history, population, attractions, events and services. Remember that they're in the business of selling the neighborhood, not criticizing it.

● **Schools and community organizations**—Visit and write local schools, organizations, clubs and businesses. Ask each for copies of its program calendar for the year. What are you competing against for the time and energy of your kids and their parents? What's important to these folks?

Other organizations' program calendars can save you time as you develop program ideas of your own. Try examining the same issues kids and parents are examining, in light of the gospel.

You also may want to tie your programs in to special school activities. And you'll avoid planning a retreat on homecoming weekend or the weekend before final exams.

● **Events**—Football games, plays, concerts, parades, pageants, speeches and meetings tell you much about the

Sample Map
of
Madeira, Ohio

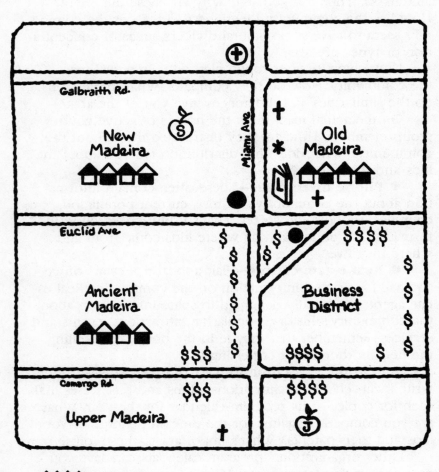

Galbraith Rd.

New Madeira

Miami Ave.

Old Madeira

Euclid Ave.

Ancient Madeira

Business District

Camargo Rd.

Upper Madeira

 Residential

$ Business/Retail

Junior High School

* My House

● Government Buildings

✝ Church

Branch Library

⊕ My Church

Elementary School

Senior High School

Map of

_____

(your community)

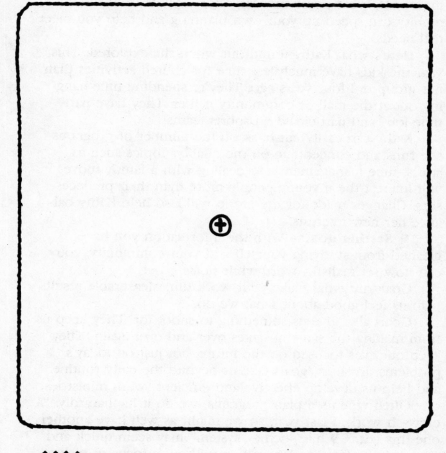

🏠🏠🏠🏠 Residential

$ Business/Retail

Ⓙ Junior High School

✱ My House

⬤ Government Buildings

✝ Church

📖 Branch Library

⊕ My Church

Ⓔ Elementary School

Ⓢ Senior High School

kids who attend. Do they arrive late or early? Do they **hang** around and talk afterward or head home? Do they enjoy themselves or do they attend out of obligation?

By observing your kids in other settings in your community you can find out what works with them (and just as important, what doesn't work). Your insights from the community can speed up your own planning and help you meet real needs.

Here's what Kathy found out when she explored: This year the kids have much less time for church activities than her group did four years ago. They're spending time hanging out at the mall or community center. They have part-time jobs and participate on sports teams.

Kathy can easily cut back on the number of programs she runs and concentrate on the quality. Topics such as stress, time management and dealing with a family move will interest these young people more than their predecessors. Changes made for the group will also help Kathy balance her new interests.

● **Setting goals**—With the information you have gleaned from studying yourself and your community, you can now set realistic, worthwhile goals.

Goals are what make your work fun. Measurable results help us feel good about what we do.

Goals also give us something to shoot for. They keep us from making the same mistakes over and over again. They keep our eyes focused on the future, not just on today's problems. In short, goals take us beyond the daily routine and help us develop effective and efficient youth ministries.

Often when we plan programs, we do it haphazardly. "A carwash worked last year, so we might as well have another one this year." While such a "system" may seem quick and easy, it isn't effective. We end up without a focus or vision. So we don't feel good about where we're heading (if we *know* where), and we don't have the creative spark that keeps us and our ministries fresh and alive.

So let's look at a simple, systematic way to organize our ministries. Every youth ministry should include the following:

● worship;
● Christian education;

● fellowship and group-building; and

● mission and service.

Your particular ministry may include other things, such as program maintenance (fund-raising and planning events), evangelism, site maintenance (taking care of the youth center), and communications (newsletters, calling chains and family ministries).

Whatever shape your ministry takes, it's important to re-examine it from time to time. Here are some simple steps you can take to invigorate your vision:

● **Evaluate the present.** Look at your program calendar. Make a copy of the "Planning Worksheet" and fill it out to measure how effectively your current program includes each emphasis. Taken as a whole, do your programs contain a balance of these elements?

● Which area of emphasis does it address? Does the calendar emphasize one area over the others? Why?

● How is the good news of Jesus Christ evident in my goals for next week? next month?

● What does my program calendar say about my faith in God?

● **Think about yourself.** Compare the programs with what you have learned about your personal style and the styles of the people you work with:

● Do the events and programs allow me to use my strengths to my group's greatest advantage?

● Do the programs, classes and events address my kids' real needs?

● Are the programs on the calendar because the kids said they wanted them? Why did the kids say they wanted them?

● Can I handle the demands these programs will put on me?

● Do I have support I can count on?

● **Include others in the process.** Finally, bring your volunteers, your youth counselors and even your Sunday school teachers into the thinking and planning processes. Encourage them to take the same inventories you've taken. Share your responses. The gifts and graces brought by these wonderful people may offset those you lack.

Planning Worksheet
Primary Youth Group Activities

	Hours Spent in Each Area During the Past Seven Months							Total Hours Spent
	Month	Month	Month	Month	Month	Month	Month	
Christian education								
Worship								
Fellowship and group-building								
Service and mission work								
Fundraising								
Other								

● **Don't stop now.** Follow this program evaluation process every year or so. It may also help you get to where you want to go.

Who Needs More Time?

Like the two pastors, it would be nice to have a year or two to ease into our youth ministry; it would be nice to take a couple of months off from programs to visit and talk to our young people. Those luxuries might fine-tune our ministry.

But they aren't necessary!

With a realistic evaluation of your own personality traits and skills as well as a broad picture of the teenagers in your community, you can carry on an efficient and effective ministry. And you can still have time to visit your kids at home, in the hospital or at football games and dances without sacrificing your sanity or your family.

CHAPTER 3

Mired in the Minutia of Ministry

Poor Pete! He just got back to the church after a day off. He's sitting at his desk wondering if this day-off business is worth the hassle.

There are 12 phone calls to return—three of them marked "urgent." The mail is stacked 3 inches deep. Scribbled memos from the church secretary, pastor, two Sunday school teachers and a parent all ask questions Pete needs to answer ASAP.

The youth minsters' association meets at noon. That'll easily stretch until 2 p.m. There's still that Bible study to plan. And tonight the youth council meets, and Pete still has to set up the chairs, make coffee, set out refreshments, type and photocopy the agenda and call Beth to ask her to take minutes at the meeting.

Besides what's due today, there's the bulletin board that hasn't been changed in three months. Pete's guitar needs new strings, the spring retreat is only three weeks away and another junior high Sunday school teacher just quit. Plus, Pete thinks he may be getting a cold.

How will he ever get all this stuff done, Pete wants to know. Things wouldn't be so bad if he hadn't taken a day off to go fishing, he's thinking. Stuff wouldn't be piled up so high.

He's wrong, of course. But that's excusable. He's upset.

Let's leave Pete in peace for a few minutes. He'll have a good cry, and when we come back, he'll be a new person. In the meantime, let's look at ways Pete and all of us can keep from getting mired in the minutia of ministry.

The Mail

Deal with the mail as soon as you look at it. I answer mine standing up. To my right is a wastepaper basket and to my left is a photocopier.

With each piece of mail I have one of three options—do it, delegate it, drop it.

Do It

Some letters and communications must be answered. Of these there are three types:

● Letters that just need a simple answer. Write your response in the letter's margin, photocopy the letter and return the original immediately. File the photocopy.

● Letters that need a little bit longer answer but nothing formal. I use post cards for these. Write the answer in longhand, photocopy the card and mail it. Staple the photocopy to the original letter and file.

● Letters that require a formal response. Remember that formal doesn't necessarily mean long. If you can't answer the letter in a single page, use the telephone instead. People probably won't read a letter that's much longer than a single page anyway.

Write a draft of your reply on the back of the letter you received. (Remember: You'll save a lot of time with the other mail, so you'll have time to do a nice job here.)

Business letters don't need to be masterful prose. They just need to state what you want to say as quickly and clearly as possible. Basically, a business letter should look like the "Basic Business Letter Format"—balanced, clean, lean, logical, simple and efficient. It takes less time to write, less time to read and less time to answer. Everyone saves.

Here are some guidelines to keep your letters short and to the point:

● Address your letter to a person by name, if at all possible.

● Write like you talk. Don't use silly business jargon such as "in re" or "enclosed please find."

● Don't be chatty. It's okay to end with a word about having a nice Christmas, but don't list what you're giving your kids.

● Double-check spelling and punctuation.

● Use lots of white space.

● Avoid sentences longer than 10 words and paragraphs longer than four sentences (six lines).

Basic Business Letter Format

Letterhead

Complete address of person you're writing letter to

Dear Somebody:

The first paragraph is a brief, informal greeting.

The second paragraph gets down to business. Here's the situation, as far as you see it.

The third paragraph says what you want or what you propose to do.

The last line includes a formal goodbye.

Sincerely,

P.S. Everyone reads postscripts. Put really important stuff here.

Delegate It

If you have a secretary, give the draft of your formal business correspondence to her or him. Let the secretary type it and send it (that's what he or she is there for). Ask to have the original back for your file.

If you don't have a secretary, you'll need to type formal correspondence yourself. It's a lot easier to do when you've got a draft already written.

Drop It

Most mail is worthless junk. Advertisements, promotions, newsletters from organizations you've never heard of, minutes to meetings you never attended.

Throw it away immediately.

If a piece of mail doesn't capture your imagination or scream to be opened, don't open it. It doesn't deserve to be read.

Catalogs may be the only exception here. I usually put all catalogs into a big file. When I need something I pull out all the catalogs until I get one with what I need.

I'll never miss the other stuff.

Still need some help in deciding what to throw away? Use this criterion: Will it have any effect on my ministry? If not, out it goes.

Telephone Calls

The telephone is a wonderful gift to youth ministry. It saves hours of running around and reams of paper. But it can also be a curse if we don't use it efficiently. The two biggest telephone time-wasters in youth ministry are messages and telephone tag.

Getting the Message

To save time returning phone messages, do two things before you ever get the messages:

● First, have whoever takes calls in the office change how he or she responds to requests for you. If you call me on my day off my secretary will say: "Dean isn't in his office today. It's his day off. You can reach him here tomorrow morning after 9."

This places the return call in the caller's court. If my secretary said: "Dean's not in his office today. It's his day off. May I have him return your call?" a lot of people would think, sure, why not. Then I'd have a ton of calls to return, many of them unnecessary.

● Second, if the call is one that you must return, have the person taking the messages *always* write the caller's phone number, when to reach the person at that number and what the call is about. Few things are as exasperating as receiving a message that says, "Call Mr. Phipps." Who's Mr. Phipps? What's his number? What does he want? When should I call him?

You'll save lots of time in the long run if your secretary gets complete information the first time:

Caller: Hello, may I speak to Dean Feldmeyer?
Secretary: Dean isn't in his office today. It's his day off. You can reach him here tomorrow morning after 9.
Caller: Could you have him call me, please?
Secretary: Certainly. May I have your name, telephone number and a time you can be reached?
Caller: This is Sarah Benchley, 555-2500. I'll be in all morning tomorrow.
Secretary: May I ask what this is regarding?
Caller: I'm with Ashbury Farm. Mr. Feldmeyer called us about a hayride for his group.
Secretary: Thank you very much. I'll see that Dean gets the message.

Telephone Tag and How to Avoid It

Telephone tag is that horrible game we've all played. I call you and leave a message because you're not there. Then you call me and leave a message because I'm not in. Then I call you back and leave a message.

Sometimes this game is unavoidable. Youth ministers don't sit behind desks waiting for calls to come in. But there are a few things you can do to cut the game short:

● From your end, have certain office hours when you're always available. These are times you set aside to be in your office to catch up on paper work and take calls. Three hours a week is usually enough. One hour in the morning on Monday and Friday and an hour in the afternoon on Wednesday works for me.

At the other end, make calls when they'll be most productive. Morning is often the best—after breakfast meetings end and before midmorning meetings begin. Lunch hour is a bust; don't even try making calls then, unless you know the person you're calling is available. Afternoons are chancy, since people are often out and about. Supper time at home is really good for catching people, but you don't make many friends by calling then.

When you return a call and the person isn't available, note on the back of the message the date and time you tried to return the call. Continue to do this each time you try. It will remind you of when it might be appropriate to try again.

● One final thought: I generally don't get too anxious about returning phone calls. It's important to be courteous and professional. But at the same time I often find that the really "urgent" calls that "absolutely require" my "immediate attention" usually take care of themselves by the time I return the calls. So, while I try to return calls promptly, I save my energy for the real crisis calls, which are forwarded to me immediately.

Memos

Memos are a pain. They're often forgotten, misplaced, unread or overwritten. Whenever possible, handle interoffice communication in person.

When you get a memo, answer it immediately like you do those letters that require only short answers. Write your answer in the margin or on the back of the memo, and return it at once.

If it requires thought and maybe some digging, do it as soon as possible to get it out of your way.

I rarely write a memo. Before I do, I ask myself if there's a better way to handle the communication. Does it concern only one person to whom I could speak individually? Can it be mentioned in a staff meeting or included in the next newsletter? Is it really that critical to communicate the information, or will my memo just be another one of many papers that clutter my colleagues' desks?

If a memo is the best way to handle the communication, use the KISS formula: Keep It Simple, Sweetheart. The "Sample Memo" shows an example.

Sample Memo

MEMO

TO: All Volunteer Receptionists   **FROM:** Dean Feldmeyer

Beginning January 15, Joan Smith will be a volunteer in the Youth Office from 1pm to 4pm on Wednesday. Please forward any calls for her to the Youth Office.

DATE: January 12

Notice in the example that I don't explain what Joan will be doing. I don't review past problems with getting phone calls through to volunteers. Those issues are best left to staff meetings. I don't mention how many kids Joan has, how old they are, or why they might call her. I don't mention who else might call her either.

And I don't make a photocopy for each volunteer receptionist. One copy posted in the reception area works.

Simple, straightforward. And it saves tons of writing, copying and distributing time.

By the way, if you want to keep the rest of the staff up

with what you're doing, send them each a copy of your
meeting minutes, calendar or program schedule with "FYI"
(For Your Information) written on the top.

If they have questions, they'll send you a memo.

Mule Work

Mule work includes all the stuff you forgot you had to
do. It's usually physical labor of some kind: setting up
chairs, making coffee, making copies, making posters,
decorating bulletin boards, sending thank-you notes.

We'll deal with some of this stuff in other chapters. But
for now, here are some hints to help you get over your
main anxiety.

● **Hint #1**—Don't do it. There's a principle that says,
"If you do it, it's your job."

If you don't set up the chairs, someone else will. Is
it really necessary that the chairs be set up exactly the way
you want them set up? Do you really need coffee at this
meeting? Is this poster necessary?

The bottom line: How much time are you giving to this
activity? Does it deserve that much time, thought and energy? If not, don't do it.

● **Hint #2**—Delegate it. Learn to ask other people for
help. I know, sometimes it's easier to do it yourself. But are
you really helping people "be the church" if you do everything for them? Even if they fail, sometimes the kindest
thing to do is let them fail and be there to pick them up afterward.

● **Hint #3**—Stop making copies. You painstakingly prepare written material for a meeting. Aren't you depressed afterward when you have to pick up and throw away all the
papers people didn't even think enough of to take home?

Stop making so many copies! Instead of duplicating the
agenda for people, write it on a blackboard or on a sheet of
newsprint, and hang it in the front of the room.

● **Hint #4**—Leave yourself time. If, after all of the
above, you've still decided you need to do the mule work,
leave yourself plenty of time. Know in advance what you're
going to do and how you're going to do it. Figure out how

much time it'll take, and leave that time in your schedule.

● **Hint #5**—Love it. Sometimes we get the idea that mule work is beneath us. We think: "Hey, I went to college. I shouldn't have to set up chairs, make coffee, shovel snow, turn on the furnace and plug in microphones."

On the other hand, our Lord washed his disciples' feet. We're called to be servants to those we lead. Often, we show our love for our kids and our work by being servants, janitors, cooks and nurses as well as teachers and preachers.

Balancing the Books

To me, keeping track of the financial records is time-consuming and distracting. I'm not trained to be an accountant—I'm a minister.

To do bookkeeping efficiently, quickly and accurately, use a ledger book (you can buy one in any office supply store) and keep it like a checkbook.

Start with a line-item budget.

Place each line item on a separate page and record deposits and deductions as they occur. When a special event requires its own bookkeeping, start a new page for that event.

After the event, photocopy the ledger page and include it in a file with the other records from the event. Next time you'll be able to see just how much everything cost and how the money came in.

I've included some sample bookkeeping pages. If you like, use them as models for your own system.

Problem-Solving

They never told me in seminary that I'd spend at least half my time solving problems. But that's how it works.

An exasperated Sunday school teacher wants to quit. A parent wants you to do something immediately about how the other kids treat her son. The janitor complains because the youth group scratched the floor in the fellowship hall. The women's group wants to know why the kids ate all the cupcakes in the fridge. The VCR is broken—again. Someone

Sample Bookkeeping

Overall Annual Budget

Total Youth Budget	$1,000.—				
1. Transportation Costs	350.—				
2. Refreshments	100.—				
3. Newsletter & Publicity Mailings	150.—				
4. Spring Retreat	100.—				
5. Equipment	50.—				
6. Curriculum Resources, Magazines, Books, Games	150.—				
7. Miscellaneous	100.—				
Total	1,000.—				

		4. Spring Retreat	Deposits	Expenses	Check #	Balance
1	1	Budgeted Funds				100.—
1	5	Deposit For Camp		75.—	#00416	25.—
1	10	Registrations (5)	175.—			150.—
1	30	Registrations (7)	175.—			325.—
2	15	Registrations (3)	75.—			400.—
3	20	Food — Payless Grocery		188.46	#01815	211.55
3	22	Film Rental		45.—	#01830	166.55
3	24	Newsprint, Markers, etc		12.18	#01878	154.37
3	24	Game Prizes		10.45	#01879	143.92
3	26	Balance For Camp		125.—	#01901	18.92
		Ending Balance				$18.92

misplaced the extension cord and no one can find it. Someone left the lids off the felt markers and they've all dried
out. The junior high Sunday school teacher is teaching the
book of Revelation instead of the Sunday school curriculum
and is scaring the daylights out of the kids.

How do you handle all the problems and still have time
to do anything else? Again, some general guidelines:

● **Give the problem time.** Especially when people
are upset, let things cool down. Do nothing right away. Today's crisis may not seem so urgent after a couple of days.

● **Be a good listener.** Some problems have no solutions; we must live with them. People usually know this,
but they want to complain to someone. And you're it.

● **Ask yourself, "Is this really a problem?"** A
problem is something that blocks us from achieving our
goals. Are you being blocked by this "problem"? Or is it
really just a nuisance?

● **Refer the problem to a committee.** If it's appropriate, take the problem to the youth council, the staff or
another similar body in your church. Ask, "What do you
think we should do?" Spreading out the responsibility not
only protects you but gives you the opportunity to delegate
the solution to the person who offers it.

● **Solve it.** If you've decided to solve the problem,
make your decision and act quickly. People may disagree
with you. But they're more likely to respect decisive leadership than wishy-washy equivocation.

● **Confront it.** Confrontation is often painful, but it's
also scriptural. If people have problems with each other,
those problems are best solved by the people themselves.
You can act as a go-between, helping them communicate
with each other.

● **Help people solve their own problems.** Help
them see the alternatives, and encourage them to pick one.
Make sure they know that you're there for them, no matter
how the situation turns out.

Mirth in the Mire

More than any other kind of ministry, youth ministry

involves details. We're required to move faster and yet be just as professional, complete and focused as any other leader in the church.

Pete (remember Pete?) may feel overwhelmed right now, but he needn't in the future. By planning ahead, he can resolve many issues before they arise. By using the suggestions here, he can cut through the dense foliage of his work and get to the important place where real ministry happens.

But minutia—details—aren't the only things that drag us down and put a burden on our time. There are important, substantive and substantial concerns that often feel like 1,000-pound weights crushing the life out of our ministry. Meetings, programs and general communication with our kids are all important parts of our work. They, too, can be cleaned up and streamlined into efficient tools for ministry.

These issues are examined in our next chapter.

■ CHAPTER 4 ■

Meetings, Meetings, Meetings

The area youth rally planning meeting is scheduled for 7:30 p.m. Wednesday. You show up at 7:25—the first to arrive. The next person comes in at 7:29, and the chairperson arrives at 7:35.

As committee members drift in, the chairperson tries to find the meeting room. (The host church member hasn't shown up yet.) One committee member tracks down felt-tip markers and newsprint. The other adults and teenagers form two circles and talk about:

Someone's surgery.	Someone's ski accident.
Someone's trip to Hawaii.	Someone's trip to the principal's office.
Someone's new baby.	Who's dating whom.
Someone's new car.	Someone's new car.
A pastor.	A pastor's kid.

Finally, the chairperson shuffles everyone into a room, and people grab chairs wherever they find them. The chairperson apologizes for not being prepared. The host church member (who finally showed up) slumps down in her chair.

The chairperson announces that there's a problem with parking at the youth rally site. Any ideas?

Larry Layman proposes using a shuttle from his church, located near the site. Wilma Worry proceeds to list all 18 reasons why Larry's solution won't work. Among her reasons is that old favorite: "We tried that once before, and it didn't work."

Sam Support jumps to Larry's defense—not because he really likes the idea, but because he's afraid to hurt Larry's feelings. But it's too late. Larry has already agreed with Wilma and abandoned his own idea, which the chairperson thought was actually a pretty good idea.

By now half the high school committee members are passing notes, and the other half are half-asleep.

Lucy Latecomer arrives (it's now 8:05) and has to be filled in on what's just happened. She suggests using a different site. Wilma Worry points out what's wrong with this idea, including, "We've never done that before." She's interrupted by Harry History, who thinks the committee should conduct a study of the problem.

And on it goes.

Someone has to leave early. Another latecomer arrives. They argue. They drift off the subject. They come back to it. Finally, they agree that the chairperson should solve the parking problem.

By now it's 10 p.m.—too late to take up any new business. So you have to plan another meeting, which is hastily scheduled after trying about 15 dates (none of them good for everybody).

□ □ □

A meeting like this wastes time. It drains creativity and energy. It saps strength and the desire to be decisive and active in ministry. And, worst of all, it's probably like most of the church meetings we attend.

Meetings can waste time when they're run poorly and/or unnecessary. Even if they don't cause burnout, they can certainly accelerate its onset.

Keys to Effective Meetings

Hard as it may be to believe, church meetings weren't invented to help us suffer for Christ. They can actually serve important purposes and serve them well. Prayer meetings, fellowship meetings, worship services, picnics, parties, work-camps—each of these meetings serves an important purpose.

Usually when people complain about meetings, they're talking about *administrative* meetings. Youth council meetings. Staff meetings. Committee meetings. Retreat-planning meetings. The list goes on. These kinds of administrative meetings are most prone to becoming time-wasters.

The purpose of an administrative meeting is to administer—to manage, to decide, to dispose of. Too often, though, we get carried away with eating, visiting, sharing or group-processing, and we forget how to make decisions. So administrative meetings are the ones I want to focus on.

All you need to straighten out administrative meetings are the old five W's you probably learned in English class. Except I'm going to rearrange them: *why, what, who, where, when.* With the correct answers to these five questions, administrative meetings can become effective tools for our ministries.

Why Meet?

As important as goals and agenda are to a meeting, they're not the reason to meet. If our purposes are to solve problems, set dates, establish programs and make decisions, we wouldn't need meetings. One person can do these things more efficiently (and probably better) than a committee.

The real purpose of any meeting is to develop *group ownership.* The reason we have meetings is to let people participate in the decision-making process. And, through their participation, they can gain a sense of ownership in the decisions we make. A decision made in a meeting is not "his" or "her" decision. It is "our" decision. It reflects "our" thinking and "we" stand behind it.

What to Do?

Long before the meeting, determine it's goals. State goals in measurable terms so you'll know whether you've achieved them when the meeting concludes.

Goals for an administrative meeting should be:
● realistic, given the time available;

- achievable, given the resources available; and
- measurable.

At the end of the meeting you should be able to say: "We needed X before the meeting. Do we have X? Yes."

Preface each goal with the phrase, "At the end of the meeting we will . . ."

Here are some examples:

- At the end of the meeting we will . . . have a date and place for the spring picnic.
- At the end of the meeting we will . . . have someone scheduled to lead games at the picnic.
- At the end of the meeting we will . . . have someone scheduled to bring the food to the picnic.
- At the end of the meeting we will . . . have a chair-person for the calling committee.
- At the end of the meeting we will . . . have the name of a person to recruit drivers for the summer mission trip.

When determining goals, remember that an *administrative meeting* is no place to plan or deal with details. Some fine-tuning may occur, but this meeting should be more concerned with the big picture than with details.

Generally, if something has to be created—a written report, a policy statement, a program outline—leave this job for another time. Groups can make decisions, but the creative process is too complicated to give to a whole group of people. Even small groups (two or three people) may have trouble handling details unless they've worked as a team for a long time.

Let an individual or small group (no more than three people) do the initial work. Then let the committee fine-tune the product for its purposes.

For instance, if you ask a committee when and where to hold the spring picnic and what to do at the picnic, you're asking for trouble. Everyone will have an opinion. Committee members will spend hours discussing this one item, ignoring the rest of the agenda.

Better to say to the committee: "The picnic committee suggests that we have the spring picnic on Saturday, April 22, at Jefferson Park from noon to 5 p.m., and that we eat and play games and end the day with devotions."

Given this basic framework, the whole committee can fine-tune the plan. Maybe 1 p.m. to 4 p.m. would be better. Have devotions at the beginning, not the end. And so forth, without having to create the event from nothing.

Who Should Be There?

You already know *why* you are having a meeting—to create a sense of group ownership for the decisions. You know *what* you want to accomplish at the meeting—your goals.

It's left, then, to determine *who* should be there, *where* it should be held and *when* the meeting should take place.

The *who* depends on the *why* and the *what*.

Who needs to be part of the group ownership process?

Who needs to make the decisions on the agenda?

Who can best help you accomplish the meeting goals?

If you're planning youth group activities, you probably have a staff of volunteers and a select group of teenagers who should attend. Or you may want to include a loose confederation of parents and teachers who support your ministry. You may want to add some others. Remember, there's no reason to waste other people's time by asking them to attend a meeting where they won't be needed. Make an alphabetical list of those who will attend along with their addresses and phone numbers. That takes care of *who*.

Where to Meet?

Now decide where to meet. Your own leadership style and the mood you want to establish for the meeting will help determine the best location. If this is truly a business meeting—called for the purpose of doing business—then use a business setting.

Forget about comfortable couches and chairs. Use folding chairs that make people sit up and face each other. Provide tables if you expect people to write or take notes.

Decide what you'll need to run the meeting effectively. Usually, this includes a chalkboard and chalk or felt-tip markers and newsprint secured firmly to an easel. You may want to provide pencils and paper for your members. Coffee and snacks aren't a good idea unless you plan to be there a long time—and that's the last thing you want.

Business meetings in people's homes usually aren't a good idea. The mood is often too relaxed, and you'll lose one member to hosting chores. Meet at the church in a room that fits your needs. Of course, make sure the room is available for the date you need it.

Before the meeting, have the room set up in a way that's conducive to conducting business. Use the "Sample Room Setup" as a guide. If a custodian is available to setup, share the diagram with him or her. If not, give it to whoever you recruit to do the job.

When to Meet?

Your meeting time may be largely determined by your church's traditions. Some churches have only evening meetings. Others have morning meetings or Saturday meetings.

People's work schedules and school schedules will also determine the best meeting times. If you meet in the evening, make sure most members have time to get home and eat dinner before heading for the church.

Plan the meeting's ending time. Most people who attend evening meetings have already had a full day. They'll have limited energy and creativity when they arrive. And if you meet on weekends, people will have other things to do and won't want to sit in a meeting for hours on end. A 90-minute time limit is a good guideline.

Finally, realize that 100 percent attendance is rare in any administrative meeting. People have other important obligations in their lives and sometimes must miss important meetings. Don't take it personally. If someone's attendance is absolutely necessary, call that person before you set the meeting to make sure the date works.

Use the "Meeting Plan Checklist" to organize your meetings.

Sample Room Setup

⊕ = Chairs   ▭ = Rectangular table
⊥ = Chalkboard   △ = Easel with newsprint
▭ = Screen   ◼ = Projector

Meeting Plan Checklist

Use this checklist when planning your next administrative meeting.

☐ Name of organization _____
☐ Time meeting will begin_____
☐ Time meeting will end _____
☐ Location of meeting
    Address _____
    Room number _____
☐ Room use confirmed this date _____
☐ Purpose of the meeting _____
_____
_____

☐ Goals of the meeting
_____
_____
_____
_____
_____

☐ Equipment needed for the meeting
_____
_____

☐ Notification sent to members this date _____
☐ Meeting process: ☐ Parliamentary ☐ Consensus
List those notified of meeting on reverse side of page.

Pulling Off a Productive Meeting

I hope you're beginning to believe that worthwhile administrative meetings can happen. You've set the stage for one. Now all you need to do is create an agenda, notify the participants and meet!

Creating an Agenda

A planned agenda tells your members that you don't call frivolous meetings. You take their time and energy seriously.

Your agenda should list the goals, activities and an approximate time schedule. I've included a "Sample Agenda" and an "Agenda Worksheet" that you can photocopy and use. Here are some brief notes on the various parts of the meeting:

● **Welcome and opening (2 to 5 minutes)**—Take a minute or two to welcome members and thank them for coming. If people aren't acquainted, have them introduce themselves.

You may want to use name tags. Or you might have people say something to help others remember their names. For example, have people each use an adjective that starts with the same letter as their first name.

"Hello. I'm Dangerous Dean."

"Hello. I'm Funny Fran."

● **Devotions (10 to 15 minutes)**—Devotions set the theological tone of the meeting. They're more than prayers. They involve Bible study and applying your faith to the business you're undertaking.

You can take several approaches to these devotions. You might use a scripture passage from the previous Sunday's sermon. Ask people to share what they see as the text's key words and images. Or use a scripture passage from next Sunday's sermon. Ask what the sermon's point should be. Or use a scripture passage from your own devotional reading. Share any insights you've gained from it.

End the devotions with a prayer asking that God's word be revealed in the church's administrative work.

● **Approval of the agenda (2 to 3 minutes)**—Present the agenda, either written on individual handouts or on newsprint in front of the room. (Remember, don't make copies unless they're essential.)

Ask if the agenda is complete. (It should be if you've prepared well.) Then ask the group to approve the agenda. With that approval, you have the group's permission to keep the meeting moving so it stays with the printed schedule.

Sample Agenda

Time	Item	Person
7:30 p.m.	Welcome and opening	Charlie Chairman
7:35 p.m.	Devotions	Rev. Goodpastor
7:45 p.m.	Approval of the agenda	

7:47 p.m. Old business

A. **Report From the Spring Picnic Committee** Farrah Foodlove
Date _____ Times _____ Location _____
Activities _____
_____

8:00 p.m. B. **Report from the After-School Bible Study Committee** Bill Bible
Day _____ Times _____ Location _____
Comments _____

8:10 p.m. New business

A. **Report From the Summer Workcamp Coordinator** Wendy Work
Dates _____ Location _____
Cost _____ Comments _____
_____

8:25 p.m. Reports from standing committees
A. Youth Choir Terry Tune

8:35 p.m. B. Sunday School Sarah Study

8:45 p.m. C. Fund-Raising Committee Bob Bucks

8:55 p.m. Closing review and Benediction
Charlie Chairman

Next meeting: Day __Wednesday__ Date __February 15__

Time __7:00 p.m.__ Location __Church library__

Agenda Worksheet

Use this worksheet to plan the agenda for your next administrative meeting.

Time	Item	Person
_____	Welcome and opening	_____
_____	Devotions	_____
_____	Approval of the agenda	_____
	Old business	_____
_____	A. _____	_____
	_____	
	_____	
_____	B. _____	_____
	_____	
	_____	
_____	C. _____	_____
	_____	
	_____	
	New business	
_____	A. _____	_____
	_____	
	_____	
_____	B. _____	_____
	_____	
	_____	
_____	C. _____	_____
	_____	
	_____	
_____	D. _____	_____
	Other business	
_____	A. _____	_____
_____	B. _____	_____
_____	C. _____	_____
_____	D. _____	_____
_____	Closing review and benediction	_____

Next meeting: Day_____Date_____

Time_____Location_____

● **Old business (time varies)**—Old business includes any reports from people who agreed to do something at the previous meeting. Again, make sure there are goals for what's being done here. Is the report being read just for form's sake? If so, forget it.

If reports tell about successes, celebrate them. How many people attended the rally? Great, let's thank God for those people by singing the doxology to the tune of "Fernando's Hideaway."

Even if a report shows that a program failed, don't let the failure dampen the whole meeting. Evaluate what needs to be changed in the future. Then thank God for the wisdom learned in failure by singing a verse of "O God, Our Help in Ages Past."

Complete old business by stating the goals of each report or item of business. Then move on.

● **New business (time varies)**—New business includes any goal that hasn't been covered in a previous meeting. List the item and the goal so the members know what's expected of them. The schedule on the written agenda tells them how much time they have to accomplish the goal.

● **Closing review (5 minutes)**—Review the goals met at this meeting. Do this for two reasons:

1. To make sure everyone is on board and knows what's going on.

2. To give everyone a sense of accomplishment at having accomplished so much at the meeting.

● **Benediction (1 minute)**—Never allow a meeting to simply fizzle. End it with authority and a sense of celebration. Literally, benediction means "good word." Close the meeting with a good word. Something taken from the opening devotion is ideal.

By following this agenda you'll have 60 to 70 minutes of a 90-minute meeting to conduct your old and new business. That's plenty of time if you plan right.

Notifying Members

Nothing wastes time like holding a meeting when nobody comes. Do your best to get the maximum number of members to attend the meeting.

Good attendance saves time because you don't have to bring people up to date on what was decided and why. You don't have to recruit because people got their assignments at the meeting. And the minutes will remind people what they agreed to do.

So do yourself a favor. Save time later by letting your members know about the meeting well in advance.

To notify members of the meeting, send them each a letter and a copy of the agenda. Your notices should be short, positive and interesting. Use humor if you can. Write a poem. Write a song they can sing to a familiar tune. Use clip art. Use bright paper.

Make sure you tell them everything they need to know in as little space as possible. The "Meeting Announcement" illustrates a simple, businesslike meeting announcement.

Meeting Announcement

Dear _____

There will be a meeting of

_____
(the committee's name)

on _____ at _____.
(date)   (time)

This meeting will take place in

_____
(room)

Our agenda is enclosed.
Please call me at_____
if you are not able to attend.   (phone)

Thank you,

_____
(your name)

P.S. If you aren't there, we'll send a big, hairy fellow with tattoos on his arms to find out why!

Add a little clip art and you have a great meeting announcement. Address the letter by hand and use a brightly colored envelope. People may even open it and read it!

Send the announcement at least two weeks before the meeting. Follow up with phone calls if you want even better attendance. (A committee member can do this.)

The Meeting

Once you've planned an agenda and notified all committee members, you're ready to meet. Everything should be perfect, right? But just in case, arrive 10 or 15 minutes early. If there's a problem you can solve it before the meeting starts.

Begin and end on time. You may have heard: "The meeting always starts 15 minutes late because the people never get there on time." People never get there on time because the meeting always starts 15 minutes late.

If you begin on time, your reputation will spread quickly, and people will show up on time. If you end on time, your promptness will keep 'em coming back.

How you run the meeting is really a matter of personal preference. There are two basic administrative methods to consider. Let's look at the two methods:

● **Parliamentary procedure**—This old standard is efficient and fast. It's based on majority rule, and its goal is to see that everyone gets a chance to speak. But it's rather stiff and formal, and many people find it intimidating if they don't know how to use it.

If you're going to use parliamentary procedure in your meetings, let everyone know in advance. Make sure they have the rules of order long before the meeting. This is especially important for young people, who most likely are not familiar with the process.

I heartily recommend this leadership style for meetings of more than 15 or 20 people. You can find good digested versions of *Robert's Rules of Order* that give the basic procedures. When using parliamentary procedure, the meeting chairperson's role is to monitor the process. He or she sees that everyone follows the rules. The chairperson isn't allowed to speak an opinion.

While this meeting style certainly has its place, it can be frustrating to those who don't know how to use the system. People may not know how to make a motion, amend a motion or defeat a motion so a new one can be made. They may feel that a proposal has been railroaded over them by people who are more interested in procedure than product.

● **The consensus method**—This is a more informal system. The leader serves as a gatekeeper, giving everyone an opportunity to speak his or her mind. The leader's most important role is to keep everyone on the subject at hand. When the leader senses that all of the options have been aired, he or she asks for someone to "venture a consensus." That is, someone makes a statement or proposes a solution that incorporates the best wisdom from each person's statements.

Decisions are made when everyone agrees to agree.

For the consensus method to work, everyone must understand that consensus is not necessarily unanimity. It is, rather, an agreement that "this solution is the best we're going to get, and we'd better accept it and move on."

The consensus method also has its problems. Some groups tend to stray from the subject. Individuals may refuse to go along with the group unless it's done exactly the way they want. Finally, it takes time for everyone to say exactly what's on his or her mind, so discussions tend to be long and circular.

On the other hand, the system's biggest gift is the sense that issues have been thoroughly explored and that the decision has the group's 100 percent ownership.

Whichever system you choose, the key is to let your group know which one you intend to use. The poorest meetings are those in which the leader tries to mix the two systems. The result is a room full of frustrated, angry people who aren't sure just what they've done.

Once you choose your method, use it with authority. Too much time is wasted in meetings arguing about methodology. Announce how you'll proceed, then proceed accordingly.

Throughout the meeting, be sure to stay on track. This

is where a strong leader is important. The best-planned meetings can still waste time if the leader allows the discussion to wander. Someone needs to be the bad guy who reminds people that this or that is not part of the agenda for tonight, or that the agenda requires the group to move on. With good leadership, your meetings are sure to be a success.

Minutes

Dispose of minutes as quickly as possible. Don't read and correct the minutes in the meeting. The secretary can make corrections later.

Anything more than a brief, written record of what decisions were made and how is a waste of time. People probably won't read more than a single page of minutes anyway.

Have a pre-elected secretary take minutes. Minutes should include the date, starting and ending time of the meeting, those present and the name of the chairperson.

Don't include the discussion or debate in the minutes. Limit the notes to a record of what happened and what was decided.

Here are two examples of minute entries, one from a parliamentary meeting and one from a consensus meeting.

- **Parliamentary:**

    Motion by John Smith to hold the spring picnic on Saturday, April 22, at Jefferson Park. Seconded. Discussion followed. Motion carried by a vote of 12 to 4.

- **Consensus:**

    Decided by consensus to hold the spring picnic on Saturday, April 22, at Jefferson Park.

If no action is taken on an item, write:

    Report from the calling committee was received. All calls made. No action taken.

After the meeting, send copies of the minutes to the members along with the announcement of the next meeting.

Meetings to Avoid

What about meetings you're *not* in charge of? I've been

to (and—I admit it—led) my share of poorly run meetings. And I've learned to avoid them at all costs.

Sometimes we need to go right to the heart of the issue. Is a meeting really necessary? Is it going to accomplish anything that couldn't be accomplished better and faster by one or two people?

The following is a list of my favorite "time-wasting meetings."

Meetings for Meeting's Sake

Have you ever attended a meeting where you wanted to say: "Excuse me. Why are we having this meeting?" If you did ask, the only reason anyone might offer is: "Well, we always have our meeting on the third Thursday of the month."

If a group meets simply because it always meets, stop! Never call or attend a meeting that doesn't have clear, concrete goals and an announced agenda.

A word of warning: You're taking a revolutionary stance if you do this. Be prepared for flack. But hold your ground. Some are convinced that you aren't doing anything if you aren't holding meetings. Under your careful teaching, they can—and will—learn otherwise. But it may be a painful lesson.

Planning Meetings

These meetings are held purportedly to plan an activity, program, event or another meeting. Actually, though, they result in few plans. Instead, you spend hours and hours of haggling, brainstorming, negotiating, what-ifing, erasing, starting over and trying again.

Your primary accomplishment is confusion.

Meeting mathematics are strange: Two people planning for one hour to accomplish something is much more efficient and manageable than six or eight people planning for four hours. Administrative meetings are for decision-making. Leave the actual planning to one or two people. And avoid meetings that try to do otherwise.

Multipurpose Meetings

I'm often invited to speak at various civic organizations and churches. I do this often enough to think that I'm pretty good at it. I always hope that my speech will be the evening's central focus.

My hopes are usually dashed when the person contacting me says: "We'll have a light lunch. Then you'll speak after a brief business meeting."

An administrative meeting in this setting had better be brief because it certainly won't accomplish anything. It can't.

Lunch. Meeting. Speaker. It's all too much for one sitting. Most likely, one or two parts of this event will be lost. Usually it's the business meeting.

Oh, you can try to accomplish business. But your effort will be wasted. People are too busy eating or visiting or listening to the speaker to shift gears and decide what to do about the food budget for the fall retreat. You'll be frustrated by the lack of progress, and you'll have to meet again anyway because you didn't get everything done satisfactorily. So you don't really save time after all. And you've wasted time that could have been spent listening to a good speaker or having fellowship over lunch.

If you must have a meeting in this setting, understand that it's for form's sake only.

Goalless Meetings

"You probably wonder why I called this meeting." You've broken the first rule of meeting attendance: Never go to a meeting that doesn't have clear goals and an announced agenda.

Meetings without goals flounder, move about, chew on this and that, ponder something else, consider and reconsider. And they never get anything accomplished.

Memberless Meetings

Ever find yourself the only person to show up at a meeting? Or maybe just you and a couple of other people?

The temptation is to go ahead and do the work or sit around feeling bad because no one showed up.

Instead of wasting your time on one of these two pursuits, go home. Try again later.

Leaderless Meetings

The leader is ineffective or there really is no leader. You hear the phrase "group process" a lot in this kind of meeting. Forget it. Group process is great in sharing and support groups, but administrative meetings must be focused and controlled by a leader.

What to Do When You're Caught

What if you're caught in one of these meetings? Take responsibility, whether you're the leader or one of the participants. Make suggestions to cut out unnecessary discussion. Call for a decision. Form committees to do legwork. Remind people when they've strayed from the point. And trust the committee process.

Do these things, and the meetings you attend will move more quickly and efficiently toward their goals.

Then, after you've done everything you can think of, remember that there's no such thing as a perfect meeting. People are people. They're often impossible to control and to move in the direction you'd have them move. Do your best. Sit through as much as you can. And remember this poem my father told me:

> When you're drowning in an ocean
> Of amendments to the motion
> And the dialogue is getting out of hand;
>
> When the arguments are raging,
> And the members are upstaging
> A commander who's reluctant to command;
>
> When the topic is so boring
> That the chairperson is snoring

And the honor of the job has lost its glow;

When you're feeling kind of bitter
'Cause they've moved to reconsider
Propositions that were passed a year ago;

You will say, "What was I thinking,
When I answered without blinking,
'Why, of course I'll take the job!' I'm such a jerk."

But reject that feeling sour
And hang in there one more hour
'Cause you never know, this might just be God's work.

■ CHAPTER 5 ■

House Calls and Other Extravagant Necessities

O n Tuesday, Tom decided to make some hospital calls. Mary Anne, a sophomore, was recovering from knee surgery at General Hospital. Bobby, an eighth-grader, was at Memorial Hospital with a fever of unknown origin.

While he was at it, Tom would stop by Rachael's house and see her. She had mono.

Tom had a meeting in the afternoon and some other work to do. So he decided to get an early start. He left for General Hospital at 9 a.m., drove 20 minutes, found a parking space, walked into the huge facility, found Mary Anne's room number and hiked to the room.

Empty.

A helpful nurse told Tom that Mary Anne was in physical therapy and would be back in about 30 minutes. Tom understood that the nurse was talking in hospital time—"30 minutes" could be anything from 10 minutes to two hours. He decided to come back later.

He walked back to the car and drove 15 minutes to Memorial Hospital to see Bobby. He found a parking space, walked into the hospital, got Bobby's room number and walked to the room.

Empty.

A nurse at the station said Bobby's fever had broken last night and Bobby went home this morning. Of course the information hadn't worked its way to the front desk yet.

Tom walked back to the car, drove 15 minutes back to General Hospital, found a parking space, walked into the hospital, went back up to Mary Anne's room and found her—in bed, asleep, exhausted from physical therapy.

What to do? Should he wake her? Leave a note and wish her well? Wait for her to wake up?

He woke her. She was glad to see him, but her drowsiness made conversation an effort. After 15 minutes he said a brief prayer and left.

On the way home, Tom stopped to see Rachael. Rachael was watching soaps on television. She had only been to youth group twice in the last year. She hardly recognized Tom. It made the visit sort of difficult. No, downright awkward. Neither knew what to talk about. Finally, tired of trying to compete with the soap operas, Tom said goodbye and left.

By the time he got back to the office, Tom was drained. He didn't feel much like doing his other work. He grabbed a burger for lunch and slogged through the rest of his day, wondering what had happened to his morning.

Tom's story is not unusual. Calling on kids takes a lot of time and often seems unproductive. When they're sick, they often feel embarrassed and vulnerable. When they're well, they're busy. It's nearly impossible to get them to sit still for five minutes.

Now, if this were a general time management book, I'd tell you to bag the visits. No respectable business person makes house calls anymore—not even doctors. That's what office hours are for.

But youth ministry is not just another respectable business. It's a *ministry*. And in ministry we practice that ancient art Jesus instituted: We visit people where they are. We go to homes, schools, hospitals. We know from experience that personal contact is the lifeblood of ministry.

Personal contact won't necessarily build a large youth

group. (Sometimes it will, but not always.) That's not the point.

Personal contact is important simply because each person needs personal ministry. A tragedy, crisis, problem, celebration—any of these events—brings with it a need for personal, one-to-one ministry.

Remember: Personal contact may be an extravagance by other people's standards. But it's an extravagant *use* of time, not an extravagant *waste* of time. In youth ministry, it's an extravagant necessity. And it can be accomplished with some efficiency.

General Time-Savers for Visitation

The overwhelming problem of youth visitation is time—especially if you have children of your own.

First, you're already busy at work. It's easy to spend all your time at the church creating programs, solving staff problems, sending mailings, and putting out a thousand little fires. It's hard to find the time.

Second, the times when most youth group kids are available are the same times your own kids are around. Youth workers often lament that they do for other people's kids what they don't have time to do for their own.

These conflicts have simple solutions that are sometimes difficult to execute. They require both discipline and a firmly objective stance toward your ministry.

The answer to the first problem (no time): *Make* time. Delegate other responsibilities. Or let them go completely if you must. Personal contacts are too important to neglect until you've taken care of everything else. Set aside a day, an afternoon or an evening each week just for visitation. Cross the time off on your calendar and don't violate it.

The answer to the second problem (your own kids): Don't make too much time for visiting. Your family is your family and your job is your job. When the job is gone, the family will still be there. Take care of those people. Make time for them. When you make a promise to your kids, put it on your calendar and don't violate it.

Personal contacts do take time. But they don't have to

waste time if they're planned and orchestrated well. To give yourself the time you need for family and for other work activities, use the following suggestions for your visits:

● **Know why you're visiting.** Calling has often been romanticized to the point where we aren't sure why we do it, except that it's always been done, and we ought to do it.

Nothing could be further from the truth.

Why are you calling on this person? What's your goal? What do you want to accomplish? Set goals for your visits. Know what you want to accomplish with each call.

Then leave when you've accomplished what you came to do. Your calls will be more productive, more focused and more concise than they might have been otherwise.

Example: Visit with John Smith, freshman, Central High.

Goal: To discover John's interests and needs. To explain our Sunday night program and to leave a copy of our newsletter.

One goal to avoid: Formal pitches for parental support for "parent night" programs. It's better to meet with small groups of parents at picnics, coffees, teas, cookouts or parents' Bible study groups. You can talk to several people at once, saving time and adding a certain amount of positive peer pressure to your appeal for parental help.

● **Schedule your visits.** There are good times and bad times to make calls. Sometimes people are willing to sit and talk. Sometimes they want to do something else. So scheduling a visit at a certain time simply because it's convenient for you may be a big mistake. Schedule calls conveniently for both you *and* the callee. Target optimum times for achieving your goals.

If you call for an appointment before you visit, you set the stage for a formal event. "The youth minister is coming!" The house may be cleaned for your arrival. Speeches may be prepared. The family might even make a snack especially for you. Or you may see a staged presentation of the person instead of the real person.

If you choose spontaneity, though, be prepared to make several trips. Catching kids at home with a few minutes to spare is a real trick. Junior high kids are usually a little easier than senior highers, but neither is a cinch.

I've found that a compromise between appointments and spontaneous visits works best. Usually, one parent keeps the family schedule (and drives the taxi and cooks). With some luck this parent can tell you the best time to find a teenager at home.

Talk to that parent. Explain who you are, what you want to do and why. "Hi, I'm Dean Feldmeyer, the youth minister at Armstrong Chapel. I'd like to stop by, welcome you to town and invite Cassandra to our youth group. When could your teenager and I have a couple of minutes together?"

Again, this approach is no guarantee that you'll catch Cassandra. But it's better than a formal or take-your-chances meeting.

● **Always phone first.** I know, a phone call takes away spontaneity. But you'll save yourself endless hours of frustration if you call just before you leave to visit someone.

Find out if the person is around. How long will he or she be there? Can he or she see you for a few minutes? A few quick questions can make it clear if the visit is going to be effective or not.

Even an appointment doesn't guarantee that a teenager will actually be home when you arrive. Football practice runs late. The boss wants her to work overtime. He forgot you were coming and slept late. A friend came by, and she took off. Even if you have an appointment, call before you leave.

● **Don't make promises you can't keep.** Don't say, "If there's anything I can do, let me know." You may not have the time, the energy or the desire to do "anything."

● **Keep accurate records.** What a terrible waste of time to visit with people, talk with them, learn about them, share your interest and, two weeks later, not be able to recall what happened during the visit.

Accurate record keeping prevents anxiety and saves time and energy. Here are seven things to do that will keep your visits organized:

1. Make notes as soon as possible after a visit—while the events and insights are still fresh in your mind.

2. Use codes and your own shorthand. No one else will

be seeing or needing the information on these cards unless you pass it on verbally.

3. Keep records confidential. Weigh carefully what information you pass on, even to other pastors and church staff people.

4. Organize your records. File cards from different types of calls separately. Or color-code them by category and file them together alphabetically. (Photocopy each type of form on a different color of paper.)

5. Use the back of the card for additional information that might be helpful later:

- Information about other family members you saw
- Information about other family members' interests and concerns
- Direct quotes that stand out in your mind from the visit
- Directions or a map that shows how to get to the house
- Important impressions you have from the visit
- What you need to do as a result of this visit

6. If needed, use more than one card per person and staple the cards together. Add extra cards for more information or subsequent visits.

7. Keep track of who makes a call. On hospital cards, put the initials of the person who made the call.

Use the forms at the end of this chapter to help organize your records.

- **Visit with authority.** I've made calls in hospitals, clinics, hospices, mental institutions, nursing homes, day-care centers, jails and prisons. At one time or another they all seemed intimidating. At other times the staffs have welcomed and supported me and my ministry.

I make calls because I'm charged by my Lord to feed his sheep. I will not be put off by busy schedules, surly administrators, arrogant doctors, nasty guards, unsupportive families or anything else the world puts in my path. "I was sick, and you visited Me; I was in prison, and you came to Me" (Matthew 25:36).

One final reminder: Visitation is an important part of your ministry, but it's only a part. You're not in competition with the youth minister down the street who makes 20 visits a week. You are called by God to faithfulness, not to win a battle with other youth ministers or with your senior pastor.

If you make two visits per week, total, you'll have made 100 calls in a year's time. Besides that, you'll have made personal contacts by phone and at school and community events. You'll have sent cards and letters. You'll have been to retreats, camps, parties and dances.

Plan your visits. Keep neat records. And don't berate yourself too harshly for the visits you don't make. Then you'll have a well-balanced youth ministry. Youth ministers make two basic types of personal contacts: hospital and sick calls; and home visits. Understanding the special demands of each type of call will help you make them more efficiently and effectively.

Hospital and Sick Calls

Hospitals intimidate people. They're full of sick people and people who speak a mysterious language called "medicine." You can get lost for hours if you don't know your way around. Communication moves slowly. Often volunteers don't know what nurses know, who don't know what doctors know.

When you make a hospital visit, remember you're there for a legitimate and important reason. As a minister you have a right and responsibility to be there. You're participating in the care of a sick or injured person.

Here are some pointers to help you make your hospital calls move quickly and efficiently.

● **Plan your visits in the afternoons.** Doctors' hospital rounds and many treatments are scheduled in the mornings. Your chances of catching patients in their rooms are vastly improved if you go in the afternoon.

Try to avoid visiting hours. If you represent your church or are a member of the clergy most hospitals will welcome your visit any time, depending on the circumstances. Hospitals respect a minister's role in the healing process, and they give ministers more access to their hospitalized parishioners. Leave visiting hours for family and friends.

● **Coordinate your calls.** Make hospital calls together. Visit several people—even several hospitals—on the same day. Hospital visits can be emotionally and physically draining. It's usually best to psych yourself up for them all at one time. Also, driving, walking, finding your way around and so forth can take lots of time. It's best to condense the time into a single trip.

● **Demand privacy.** Your visit is important, and your time is valuable. Ask the person you're visiting to turn off the television. And if you're going to have prayer with the patient and an aide is cleaning the room, it's perfectly okay to say, "Will you excuse us for a minute, please?"

If you adopt these same suggestions for visiting teenagers who are sick at home, your visits will go quickly, efficiently and well.

● **Pray with people.** If, for some reason, a prayer time feels awkward or you aren't sure if the patient wants to pray, just ask, "Would you like to pray together?" And ask what the person would like you to pray for. Prayer doesn't have to come at the end of the meeting. Pray when it feels appropriate.

● **Use cards and the phone.** Illnesses and injuries happen unexpectedly. Sometimes you won't have the time to get to the hospital or sick bed. A phone call or a get-well card can't take your place, but it can do wonders in your absence.

● **Visit on a schedule.** How often should you make hospital calls? That's a hard one to call. It depends on a lot of variables. How ill is the patient? How long do doctors predict the hospital stay will last? What's the prognosis? Will the person spend a long time in bed after the hospital stay? How much time can you invest in visiting one-to-one?

A general rule: Visit a teenager once for every 48 hours he or she spends in the hospital.

● **Share the calls.** Personal contact from the church need not always be from the youth minister. Youth counselors or youth group members can make these visits as well. Some of the visits should be made by the church's senior minister or by the minister of visitation, if there is one.

For a person who spends 10 days at the hospital, then, provide at least five visits. They could be divided something like this: youth minister, 2; senior minister, 1; youth counselors, 1; and group members, 1. If different people visit, the visited person feels the entire church's support, not just yours, whose job it is to visit.

Home Visits

Home visits are probably more common than hospital calls (at least, we hope so). But they present unique challenges. Kids aren't home. Kids are uncomfortable having you in their home. Kids go to so much trouble getting ready for your visit that you're embarrassed to ask to come.

Let's look at the main types of home visits you make and how to make them with as little frustration as possible.

New or Potential Members

Depending on where you live and what happened before you took the job, a visit may or may not be expected. The importance of this type of visit depends on you, your community, its traditions and expectations.

If you do make these kinds of calls, follow a few simple guidelines:

● **Have a goal.** Know what you want to accomplish with the visit. Do you want to get a commitment to a specific program? Do you want to tell the person about your youth group? Or do you just want to get acquainted?

● **Take something with you** that you can leave behind: a newsletter, brochure, calendar—even a cake or pie isn't out of the question.

● **Be brief.**

● **Ask questions.** Learn about the person. Be a good listener.

● **Don't overwhelm** the person you're visiting with programs. It's better to invite people to a specific program than to overwhelm them with a whole smorgasbord of dates and times.

● **Follow up** with a card or note thanking the person for the visit and his or her time. If you invite someone to an event, follow up with a phone call from a group member.

Follow up a recruiting call with a card or a brief letter. For efficiency, I use pre-printed post cards. On one side is a cartoon character or a caricature of me shaking hands through a door. On the other side I write a note to the people I visited, thanking them for their time and inviting them to our group.

For example:

Dear Tom—Really enjoyed our visit yesterday. Hope to see you on a Sunday night real soon. Good luck with the ball game on Friday night!

Sincerely, Dean

It's effective and it only takes about two minutes.

Inactive Members

Calling on inactive members is, perhaps, the most awkward kind of visit. The inactive teenager probably has a reason for not being at church, and it's bound to put one of you in an awkward position. You, because you or another group member might have done something that has alienated the teenager. The teenager, because the reason may involve misplaced priorities.

These visits are easiest when you're new in the church. But even if you've been in your church for a while, you can still do them with grace, enthusiasm and a little planning. Here are some hints:

● **Call first.** Call the parent in charge of the family schedule and find out when would be a good time to find "Tim" at home . . . "just to stop by and say hello . . . do a little catching up. Our schedules have been so full we haven't seen each other in a while . . ."

Sometimes this phone call can answer your concern. You may find out that the group member has had a legitimate excuse for missing the past four meetings and will miss yet another before he or she can return.

● **Don't attack.** Don't approach the visit as a "Where

have you been?" call, but as a chance to re-establish a broken-down relationship.

● **Don't wait too long.** Don't let kids become inactive too long before you make this call. A month of inactivity is the most I let go by before I make contact.

● **Be ready to address concerns.** You may discover that some fence mending needs to be done. Kids leave youth groups for a lot of different reasons: They break up with a sweetheart who still attends the group. A sharp word is said. The program emphasizes something they're not good at. They're too tired, are too busy or have a schedule conflict. Their sweetheart goes to another church. They have a theological difference. They need a different worship style.

Some of these reasons are legitimate; some aren't. Some you can do something about; some you can't. Personal contact can tell you how to handle each situation effectively and efficiently.

Active Members

I visit active members because I visit inactive and new members. I can't afford to let my active members feel that I take them for granted or appreciate them only as "group members."

A personal contact makes an active group member feel valued as an individual. It creates a personal relationship outside the group setting.

Don't use these visits for business or for recruiting someone to do a job. Save those goals for another time. Visit just because the teenager is a special group member who deserves personal attention.

Here are some tips to make the most of active-member visits:

● **When to visit.** I know one youth minister who visits every kid in the group—active or inactive—on that young person's birthday. I haven't been able to pull this off, but I think it's a neat idea.

When you visit on a kid's birthday it proves that you don't have an agenda. You aren't there to recruit. You're simply there to spend a little time in celebration, in fellowship and in joy with a person you care about.

Calling on birthdays may prove to be too demanding for your schedule. So try calling on each person during the week of his or her birthday. Take a flower, a helium balloon, a card or an origami crane (it symbolizes good luck and health).

• **What to talk about.** When you talk with the person, keep conversation light. What was the past year's highlight? What accomplishment are you most proud of? What was the funniest thing that happened this year? What do you want to accomplish next year?

• **Ending the visit.** Close your visit with a prayer. Thank God for the gift of life and the gift of the previous year. Then ask for God's guidance in the next. The whole visit shouldn't take longer than 15 minutes.

Another colleague welcomes his group members home from vacation every year with a little "Welcome Home" sign in their yard. Then he shows up the following week to hear all about the vacation and look at the snapshots.

Another friend simply calls on one active member each week. She calls these her "evaluation" calls and has a series of questions she asks about the youth group.

• **Other contacts.** Finally, don't miss opportunities to call on active kids "where they are." Kids are often hard to catch at home. A brief contact such as a pat on the back, a hug, a hello, a smile or even a wink—at a ball game, dance, concert or play—can be meaningful.

It's contact. It's personal. It shows that you care about this person—as an individual. And it can be accomplished efficiently.

Keeping Perspective

Regardless of how well we plan, pastoral calls won't always be "efficient" uses of our time. We might be able to *do* a lot more if we didn't visit.

But the goal of pastoral calls is different. Our effectiveness isn't measured in numbers and it isn't determined by the *place* visited. It's determined by our professionalism, our goals for the call and the presence of the Holy Spirit.

Hospital and Sick Calls (sample)

Name: DAVID BROWN — Age/grade: SOPH

Hospital or location: GENERAL — Room: 2201

Diagnosis: TORN LIGAMENTS IN R. KNEE — F-BALL

Treatment: SURGERY 9/27 ↗

USE YOUR OWN CODES

INITIALS OF PERSON MAKING THE CALL

Date	Record of visit
9-28	DEF -- SOME PAIN, GOOD SPIRITS, TIRED
9-29	RJM -- P.T. TODAY, CRUTCHES, HOME 10/2

BE BRIEF

Hospital and Sick Calls

Name: _____ Age/grade: _____

Hospital or location: _____ Room: _____

Diagnosis: _____

Treatment: _____

_____

Date	Record of visit
____	_____
____	_____
____	_____
____	_____
____	_____
____	_____

New or Potential Member Visit (sample)

Name: *MARY KLINE*   Date of visit: *4/24*
Address: *1432 W. NESBIT*   Phone: *555-4367*
School: *CENTRAL HIGH*   Grade: *SOPH.*
Parent(s) and occupation(s): *DAVID -- SALES REP;*
JoANNE -- REALTOR
Siblings: *PETER*
Interests: *CHEERLEADER, CHOIR, STUDENT GOV'T.*
Record of visit: *SOPH AT CENTRAL HI. SHOWED ME*
NEW HOUSE -- VERY PROUD. LIKES BOYS. WAS
SEMI-ACTIVE AT PREVIOUS CHURCH IN MASS.
"I'LL TRY TO COME."
Conclusions: *LEADERSHIP POTENTIAL VERY BUSY*
Follow up: *CARD 4/25. MAIL LIST.*

ONLY PRIORITY INTERESTS

PARENTS' OCCUPATIONS ARE HELPFUL

KEEP REALISTIC

New or Potential Member Visit

Name: _____ Date of visit: _____

Address: _____ Phone: _____

School: _____ Grade: _____

Parent(s) and occupation(s): _____
_____

Siblings: _____

Interests: _____

Record of visit: _____
_____
_____
_____

Conclusions: _____

Follow up: _____

Inactive Member Visit (sample)

Name: _Susan Jones_ Date of visit: _5/31_
Address: _1431 Euclid_ Phone: _555-3265_
School: _Central_ Grade: _Jr._
Parent(s) and occupation(s): _Ron -- Dentist; Judy -- Home_

Siblings: _David -- Soph. Karen -- 7th Gr._
Interests: _Choir, Academics_
Past activities: _Semi-Active Mem., Irregular Attn., Winter Retreat_
Reason for inactivity: _Too Busy, Other Interests_
Record of visit: _15 Min. -- She Had To Leave. Talk -- Very Pleasant, Bright, Fun_
Conclusions: _Stay In Touch_
Follow up: _Card 6/2. Keep On Mail List._

(margin note, upper right) FIND OUT BEFORE THE VISIT SO YOU'LL HAVE SOMETHING TO GET THE CONVERSATION GOING.

(margin note, left) WHAT ABOUT DAVID? SCHEDULE ANOTHER VISIT IF NECESSARY.

(margin note, left) BE REALISTIC

Inactive Member Visit

Name: _____ Date of visit: _____

Address: _____ Phone: _____

School: _____ Grade: _____

Parent(s) and occupation(s): _____

_____

Siblings: _____

Interests: _____

Past activities: _____

Reason for inactivity: _____

Record of visit: _____

_____

Conclusions: _____

Follow up: _____

Active Member Visit (sample)

Name: JOHN DARKMONT   Date of visit: 3/29
Address: 73 W MAIN   Phone: 555-3606
Occasion for visit: BIRTHDAY

Goal of visit: DISCOVER HIS GIFTS ◁ ─────────┐ DON'T RECRUIT
Record of visit: TOOK BALLOON. SANG AT DOOR   BUT FIND OUT
JOHN VERY SURPRISED -- VERY HAPPY. 20 MIN. STAY WHAT HE HAS TO
                                                 OFFER

PUT FOLLOW UP PLANS ON THE BACK OF CARD

Conclusions: JOHN MAY BE AN OFFICER IN THE GROUP
NEXT YEAR. GOOD POTENTIAL. BRIGHT. GOOD LOOKING.

Active Member Visit

Name: _____   Date of visit: _____

Address: _____   Phone: _____

Occasion for visit: _____

_____

Goal of visit: _____

Record of visit: _____

_____

_____

_____

_____

Conclusions: _____

_____

_____

_____

CHAPTER 6

Taking Care of Your Volunteers

M arsha is planning a typical youth event—a carwash. First she considers publicity for the workers. She needs to tell them about it: when it is, where, what the money will be used for, what time to be there, when to expect to be home. Oh, and bring buckets, towels, and sponges.

Then there's general publicity: announcements in the church newsletter, Sunday morning bulletin, posters in the halls, community posters, maybe even a notice in the local newspaper and on a couple of radio stations.

She needs to gather supplies: extra sponges, hoses, attachments for the hoses, extra towels, extra buckets, signs for the day of the event.

For setup, she plans to be there an hour early. Signs in place. Hoses hooked up and dragged out to the parking lot.

Lunch! Oh no! Okay, have the kids bring a couple of bucks, and send someone for pizza. Better put that in the publicity.

She'll need supervisors. Water fights are part of the fun of a carwash. But she needs someone to keep people working when the cars get backed up. Call some adults.

Cashier. Get change and a cash box. Don't forget to set up a table.

Cleanup. Can't have all that mess laying around on Sunday morning. Stay an extra hour.

How much do we charge? Should we have a bake sale at the same time? Extra money there!

And what about Marsha's own family? Little Jimmy has a Little League baseball game at 10 a.m. and Jill wants to spend the night with a friend.

Of course, Marsha tries to do all this herself. She's good at her job. She'll probably get it all done, and the kids will make a million dollars. The congregation will be amazed at how talented and organized she is. Jimmy will win his baseball game with a grand slam in the bottom of the ninth, and Dad will pick up Jill at her friend's house, and . . .

And Marsha will never, ever want to do another carwash.

She'll be tired before it begins. She'll be anxious and short-tempered during the whole thing. She'll feel guilty because she missed Jimmy's grand slam. And she'll be burned out within six months.

No matter how good she is, Marsha can't do it all. She needs help. She needs to delegate some of this work. She needs someone to organize the entire event. Or, at the very least, she needs a group of people, each of whom will take small jobs so she can forget about them. (The jobs, not the people.)

Even if she could do it all and liked doing it, she shouldn't. It's not fair to her or the volunteers she works with. One day Marsha will be gone. If she does everything herself, her church's youth ministry will collapse.

One of the most effective ways to avoid burnout in youth ministry is to recruit, train and take care of a committed staff of adult youth workers. Recruiting and training are the easy parts. Taking care of volunteers is where we often fall down.

Recruiting Volunteers

Sometimes the church has an unwritten rule: "If you will, you can."

You need someone to do something in the church. So you get the membership list and start down the columns making phone calls. You hope someone will say yes. That's the first requirement. If the person is willing you assume he or she is able.

Nothing could be further from the truth.

When you recruit volunteers you need more than warm bodies. You need people who are blessed with some aptitude for the work. You need the best people you can get!

Make a list of the 10 people in your church who are—in your judgment—best suited to youth work. Let nothing except their qualifications enter your consideration as you make the list. Don't say to yourself, "She'd be great, but she's too busy." Let people decide for themselves.

1. _____	6. _____
2. _____	7. _____
3. _____	8. _____
4. _____	9. _____
5. _____	10. _____

When you've made your list, visit these people in their homes. Be bold. Ask them to give one year to youth ministry. Let them know how you came up with their names. Ask them to say no to other commitments for the sake of the kids. Tell them that without them the ministry will go on, but not as well.

Ask for a commitment. Let them think about it a few days, but call back within a week. You're doing important work. Don't apologize for it.

If they say no, thank them. Then find out why. Things may change in the future, making them available. Keep a record of this call just as you would any other (see Chapter 5).

Training Volunteers

Effective training keeps volunteers excited and ready to tackle new responsibilities. Without it, they may feel overwhelmed, discouraged and incapable.

Of course, you'll want to take advantage of all the resources from your denomination and from interdenominational sources. Today there are more how-to books, idea books, game books, magazines, workshops, seminars, camps, schools and training resources available than ever before.

One good resource is *Training Volunteers in Youth Ministry,* a video training program from Group Publishing.

Use what's available. Send your volunteers to events. Provide money in your budget to help with their expenses. Keep your library up to date.

From time to time, however, you'll need to conduct your own training. Usually, the old five-step educational process is best. It goes like this:

Step 1: I tell you how to do it.

Step 2: I do it and you watch.

Step 3: We do it together.

Step 4: You do it and I watch.

Step 5: You do it.

This method will work with anything from teaching kids how to paint with a roller to teaching adults how to lead games. Use it to train your volunteers in the activities that are unique or special to your youth group.

Taking Care of Volunteers

You've recruited great people. You've given them excellent training. But why do they burn out?

Volunteer youth workers are often beset with the same problems as their professional leaders. They're energetic, talented, capable, caring, Christian people.

But because they're so capable, your best youth workers may find themselves buried in responsibilities. They try to do everything as well as they would do one thing. They get tired. They get discouraged. They burn out.

Signs of Burnout

As a leader, it's important for you to know the signs of burnout in your volunteers:

● **Depression**—Things that were important don't seem to matter any more. The person may be unable to focus on one thing. Sadness and sarcasm often mix.

● **Fatigue**—Usually energetic, this person seems tired and bored. Physical movements will be slow and dragging.

● **Lethargy**—They'll be unable to get started.

● **Physical appearance**—A change for the worse may occur.

● **Tardiness**—They'll show up late and/or leave early.

● **Avoidance**—The depressed people may avoid you. They know they're not doing what they said they'd do. They feel guilty and embarrassed about it. But they don't know what to do.

When You See Burnout

Here's what you can do when you sense that volunteers are burning out:

● **Confront the problem.** Ask them: Are you tired? Do you feel like you're burning out? Burned-out workers are often praying that someone will see their stress and offer some help.

● **Talk about it.** Find out what brought it on and how it feels. Let the volunteers know that you know what it's like. Tell them you're there to help—not because you need them to work, but because you care about them.

● **Encourage them to take time off.** Give them a break. Cancel the youth group meeting for a week. Get a substitute. Give them time to rest.

● **Change their job.** Maybe a volunteer needs a change of scenery. A move from Sunday school to youth group may be all it takes.

● **Pray with them.** Through prayer we can find the strength, insight and courage to continue even when things seem to be too much for us.

Preventing Burnout

Of course, the best way to deal with burnout is to avoid it. Here are some ways to avoid burnout with your volunteers:

● **Be forthright.** When you recruit volunteers, tell them everything—expectations, commitments, problems, joys, satisfactions. Provide detailed, accurate job descriptions. Suggest that they talk to their predecessor. Not only is this honesty fair, but it's the only way to be sure they're aware of what's involved. People who don't have the time or energy won't accept. And you won't have to deal with their burnout three months later.

● **Teach time management.** Before they begin working with the kids, help volunteers take an inventory of their current commitments and responsibilities. How much time can they realistically give to youth ministry? Make sure they think about all their commitments—family, church, school, work, friends, self.

Once you understand volunteers' needs, keep your demands well within their limitations. Let volunteers know early what you need from them. Plan far in advance so they have time to prepare.

● **Encourage limitations.** When I recruit volunteers for youth work I ask them to say no to everything else in the church for the entire time of the commitment. I explain that their role in the youth program is that important. It can't be a halfhearted effort. It needs their full attention and energy. I tell them everything it will involve—training, education, work, recreation.

● **Build a supportive community of adults.** People volunteer for youth work for lots of reasons. One of the most popular is to be with the other adults who work with teenagers. Often they're about the same age, or have children the same age, or just have things in common with each other.

So spend time together as adults without the young people. Have cookouts. Take family retreats. Celebrate special occasions. Go shopping together. Invite each other over for dinner. Go to brunch after Sunday morning worship.

Also, be sure your youth workers can participate in adult activities in the church. All too often youth workers get shuffled off with the kids. How often I've heard the phrase "What about including Dean and the kids?" when a group was planning a churchwide event.

● **Schedule regular time off.** Even the most dedicated volunteer needs a break. And the youth group isn't going to die if you skip a week here and there to give volunteers a break. Schedule a movie party or a special event that doesn't require all the adult volunteers to be present. Let some of them take the night off.

● **Provide continuing education.** Make sure your staff has a constant input of new ideas. Begin the year with a training event, and schedule more training at various times throughout the year.

Don't let people fall into the rut of, "I've done everything I know how to do and said everything I have to say."

● **Let them fail.** Jumping in to save the day doesn't help you or your staff. When failure comes—and it will—be reassuring and encouraging. Christian teenagers don't suddenly become ax murderers because one program flops.

Evaluate what went wrong and how to avoid the problem next time (if it's possible). Then turn it over to the Lord, thanking him for the experience. And move on.

● **Trust the volunteers.** You recruited them because you felt they could do the job. Let them do it. They probably won't do it exactly the way you would. But is that really important?

● **Trust God.** God has been using people to bring his message of love and faithfulness to others since the beginning of time. He'll use these people too.

If God can use David, Rahab, Paul and Peter, then he can use your church's imperfect, not completely trained, often overworked, usually underappreciated volunteer youth workers.

And Finally . . .

When I was in high school I mowed yards for my summer spending money. I was quite a businessman, with my ledgers and tally sheets and schedules and all. It wasn't bad work and it paid well. I could even take a few days off and hire substitutes if I wanted.

After two years of mowing with my dad's old hand-push rotary mower, I decided to buy my own power mower. I saved the money, went to an auction and bought a little, used lawn mower.

I thought I was in heaven. In a couple of weeks, I nearly doubled my business by mowing more lawns, faster than I ever imagined.

Then one day I was mowing along and the mower began making a terrible, clanging, grinding noise. I shut it down. It coughed, belched blue smoke and died with a shudder. It wouldn't start.

I pushed it home and asked my dad what he thought was wrong. He bent over and started turning a little thing I'd never noticed before. He took it off and pointed down at the hole, which was issuing blue smoke from the engine area.

He shook his head. "You have to oil 'em, Dean," he said.

Oil? *Oil?* No one had ever told me anything about oil! My mower was ruined, and all because I hadn't oiled it properly?

Does it seem crass to compare youth ministry with a machine? Maybe it is. But think for a minute.

Machines don't take away the work. They just make it a little easier and quicker . . . if you take care of them.

Your volunteer staff will take care of you, but only if you keep the machinery well-oiled with good training, constant care and prayer.

By taking care of your staff, you take care of yourself. You create a supportive community. You've got a group of people who can free you to do ministry in ways you never imagined.

Take time to be good to them, and life will be good to you.

...

Taking Care of Yourself

CHAPTER 7

How to Say "No"

Marietta was a young, attractive, energetic businesswoman and mother of two small children. I felt fortunate to have her as a youth ministry volunteer.

But when she came into my office she looked tired. Her hair was uncombed, she'd lost weight and there were bags under her eyes.

She spoke hesitantly.

"I don't know where to start. I feel so harried," she said, slumping into a chair. "I've got the youth stuff to do. I'm the program chairperson for the women's group. I'm on the Christian education committee. I have choir practice every Wednesday night. My kids need more and more time. And I hardly ever see Dave anymore.

"I think I've bitten off more than I can chew."

A knot formed in my stomach. I knew what was coming. I was the youth minister, after all. If something had to go, I knew what it would be.

"No one told me!" she complained, with a hint of anger in her voice. "Every time people ask me to do something, they assure me that other folks will help me out. 'Just a couple of meetings,' they say. I've been to three meetings this week! And next week doesn't look any better!"

I tightened my grip on my chair. Here it comes, I thought.

"I just came to tell you," Marietta continued. "I wanted you to know before I resigned . . ."

There. She said it. The "r" word. I knew it. I knew it. I

knew it. My thoughts raced. What was I going to do? How could I ever replace her? The kids in the youth group would be so . . .

". . . I'm quitting the choir and the women's group."

Wha . . .?

"I'm sorry. I know they'll be mad at me. But I just can't give up the kids."

This is a dream, right? I'm having a dream. It must have been the linguine with clam sauce. Or maybe the spumoni.

"Well, I feel a lot better getting it off my chest." She was still talking. "Would you see to it that the right people get these resignation letters? Thanks, Dean. I really appreciate your support."

I sat there holding the two neatly typed letters, a big self-satisfied grin on my face. She wasn't quitting the youth group! Oh, happy day! She wasn't leaving me in the lurch! Thank you, Lord!

But wait a minute. What about the choir? Marietta has a really nice alto voice. It would be greatly missed. And what about the women's group? Who would plan the programs? Oh, no.

More problems.

Can you relate to Marietta? So many commitments. So many meetings. So many plans. So little energy. Yes, most of us have trouble saying no.

□ □ □

The Trouble With Not Saying "No"

We hate to say no.

We like to think of ourselves as bright, capable, talented and indispensable. And the church wants us to believe that. It wants us to be as involved as we can be.

But often we don't know the limits of our involvement until we've crossed them.

A major signal that we can't say no is our stress and overcommitment. And while most of us work better with a little stress in our lives, too much stress can harm us physically and emotionally. It can damage our relationships with our family and friends. It can keep us from doing well the things that are really important to us.

To test your level of commitment, take the "Should-I-or-Shouldn't-I? Quiz." Add up your yeses and see how you did.

If you answered yes to more than five of the questions, you're probably too busy to say yes to another commitment.

If you answered yes to more than eight of these questions, you're probably on the verge of serious burnout.

It's time to learn how to say no.

How does it happen? How do we get overcommitted? Here are some of the factors.

Success Breeds Success

There's a general rule in the church: If you can succeed in youth ministry, you can succeed in anything.

Generally it's true. If you can create publicity that brings out kids, you can create publicity that'll bring out anybody. If you can create programs that entertain and educate teenagers, you can create programs for just about anyone. If you can get kids to sing, you can get anyone to sing.

Small wonder that when a difficult task arises, someone gets a gleam in the eye and says, "I know someone who can do that . . ."

You don't think it's true? Try this: Write the names of your three best youth counselors. Next to their names, write three church jobs they could handle.

1. _____

2. _____

3. _____

Not hard, was it? Case dismissed.

Everybody Wants to Be Somebody

"Anne, we have a very important job we need you to do. Frankly, you're the only person who could do it the way it really needs to be done."

Sound familiar? Whoever asks may even repeat the litany

Should-I-or-Shouldn't-I? Quiz

Yes No

1. Did you spend more than three evenings at the church in any of the past three weeks? ☐ ☐

2. Have you missed more than two important personal events you wanted to attend in the past month? ☐ ☐

3. On the average, are you sleeping less than seven hours per night? ☐ ☐

4. Are you the primary leader (chairperson, president) of more than two organizations? ☐ ☐

5. Does your job require you to work more than 50 hours per week? ☐ ☐

6. Do you say "five more minutes" more than twice when it's time to get out of bed in the morning? ☐ ☐

7. Did you eat fast food because you didn't have time to cook a meal more than twice in the past week? ☐ ☐

8. Did you read fewer than four books for pleasure in the past year? ☐ ☐

9. Did you spend less than 90 uninterrupted minutes talking to your spouse or special friend last week? ☐ ☐

10. Have you gained or lost more than 10 pounds in the past two months without trying? ☐ ☐

11. Have you skipped Sunday morning worship more than twice in the past six weeks? ☐ ☐

12. Do you have high blood pressure? ☐ ☐

13. Do you experience insomnia or feel "tired all the time"? ☐ ☐

14. Have you been avoiding people from the church recently? ☐ ☐

15. Are you more short-tempered than usual? ☐ ☐

of your talents, abilities and past successes. From listening, you might be convinced that the life of the church—not to mention the kingdom of God—may rest on your completion of this job.

Flattering? Sure it is.

We want to count. We want to think we're important, invaluable—even essential.

No wonder we say: "Well, okay. I'll do it."

If you're not convinced that this happens, name three things you have said yes to in the past year that you didn't really want to do but thought you should.

1. _____
2. _____
3. _____

It's Important Work

The church's work is important. It's the most important work in the world. For all the mistakes the church has made, it has also racked up some impressive successes.

Who can count the hospitals, orphanages, nursing homes, schools, clinics, hunger programs and other helping agencies we've created? How many lives have been saved? How many marriages? How many souls have been comforted in times of hardship, anguish or despair? How many have heard the healing, comforting, liberating, invigorating, saving word of Jesus Christ? All because of the church.

Name three service organizations in your community that wouldn't operate if Christian people didn't volunteer their time and effort.

1. _____
2. _____
3. _____

Who knows what lives will be touched and changed because you give your time? Isn't it worth the effort?

Sure it is. So what if the other 23 hours of the day are already booked? If you have an hour to give, give it. Right?

The Call of the Gospel

Aren't Christians called to sacrifice? to give of ourselves?

Doesn't our Lord require us to take care of each other? feed the hungry? teach the children? make joyful noise? pick up our crosses and follow him?

Yes! The kingdom of God really is at hand. It doesn't come to us because we sit back and wait. It comes because we march forward into it, armed with our courage, faith, hope and love.

Write three scripture passages that call us to service.

1. _____
2. _____
3. _____

Drawing the Line

There's much truth in these reasons for not saying no. We *are* called to serve. We *can* succeed in many areas. We *do* want and need to be an important part of the big picture. The church's work *is* important.

But where do we draw the line? At what point do we say, "This I will do and no more." How much do we owe ourselves and our families? In short, how do we say no?

The Art of Saying No

Basically, I'm a yes person. When my children ask if they can do something, I usually say yes unless there's a compelling reason to say no.

What's more, I like yes people. They're easy to get along with. They're also easy to recruit.

Since you're in youth ministry and you're reading this book, you're probably a yes person too. You have trouble saying no. You have to have a really good reason. And in the church, all the reasons we hear seem to point toward saying yes to everything.

Why Say No?

Before we can deal with the how of saying no, we must

deal with the why and when.

● **We can't do everything.** If we can succeed in youth ministry, we can probably succeed in *anything*. But we can't succeed in *everything*.

The church can only succeed through the power of the Holy Spirit and the work of *all* the church's members. Let the church be the church. We do no one any favors by doing all the work that needs to be done.

One of the hardest things to do is let people fail. But fail they must if they're to grow and learn. How many times do babies fall before they learn to walk? Similarly, a couple of programs may need to fail before the church does its own walking.

● **Not all things are equal.** The church's work is important. But every single item is not equally important. Some things are more deserving of your time and effort than other things.

Is the paint color in the church's nursery as important as the youth retreat program? Do you have to get fresh doughnuts for the men's breakfast? Could the men eat day-old doughnuts so you could spend your time doing something more important?

What are you going to contribute to that meeting next week? Could your thoughts be sent in writing? Is it really important enough that you give up the time with your spouse? your children? your friends? your dog? So you're the publicity chairperson. Do you have to attend a meeting to do that? Can't someone get the information to you so you can do your publicity?

List all the meetings you're attending this month:

_____

_____

_____

_____

_____

_____

Now go back and arrange them in order of importance. Number them in the margin with #1 as your top priority.

Look at the lowest three priorities on your list. How

could you spend that time doing something more important? List three alternate activities:

1. _____
2. _____
3. _____

● **You are *already* somebody.** Everybody wants to be somebody. No doubt about that. The problem comes when we think that what we do makes us a "somebody." When we begin to define ourselves by how many organizations we belong to, how many committees we chair, how many programs we organize, we flirt with idolatry.

The central and indisputable fact of the gospel is that you are somebody. And it's not because of what you've done. It's because of what God has done in Jesus Christ. God has decided, determined and declared that you are somebody.

What we do doesn't determine who we are. Who we are determines what we do. So saying yes to everything isn't what makes us somebody. It just burns us out.

● **Your choices affect others.** When we're tempted to say yes, is it because we envision all the good it will do? Jobs done. Tasks accomplished. Positive feelings. But what about the negative pictures that may result from our yes?

No choice is ever ours alone. By saying yes to one thing we say no to others. Examine the total impact of your yes.

● How will it affect your family? your children? your spouse? your friends? the other people who count on you?

● Is it really fair for you to say yes to everything that comes your way? Is the body of Christ edified because you volunteer to do every job? Are there others, by chance, who want to do some of these tasks? Would others do them if you didn't rescue them every time?

● Finally, how fair are you being if you're exhausted, frazzled, tired and burned out? You end up resenting and alienating and separating yourself from others. What good are you to them then?

Contrary to popular motivational rhetoric, "Let someone else do it" can be the kindest thing to say.

● **The call of the gospel.** While the gospel calls us to sacrifice and service, it also calls us to be good and faithful stewards of God's gifts to us.

Chief among God's gifts is time. How we spend that gift witnesses to our faithfulness as stewards. The same holds true for our energy. We each have only so much. How we distribute it says much about our own faithfulness.

Look to the gospel stories. Jesus—who made the ultimate sacrifice—did so only after much prayer and soul-searching. He went into the desert alone to spend time with God in prayer and meditation. When the crowds became too demanding he retreated with his disciples to a "lonely place."

Look over these passages in Mark. Then ask yourself if you aren't expecting more of yourself than Jesus expected of himself.

● Mark 1:12-14—Jesus goes into the wilderness.
● Mark 6:30-32—Jesus and the disciples try to escape the crowds and go away on retreat.
● Mark 14:32—Jesus prays in Gethsemane.

When to Say No

I recruit people to do things. It's sometimes tempting to soften job descriptions. Twelve to 15 meetings a year become "a few meetings." Training 20 novice Sunday school teachers becomes "being a resource to teachers." Cooking all meals for 30 kids on a retreat becomes "helping in the kitchen."

And I know it's easy to assume others will help the person I'm recruiting. Well, they will, won't they? After all, this is the church.

And I know how quickly I offer my own help. "I'll be right beside you all the way" can quickly become, "Call me if you need anything."

Pastors, recruiters and nominating committees are under pressure to get a name on the dotted line. Too often the attitude is: "Find someone who'll do the job. Worry about the problems later."

As a potential recruitee, you need to be aware of those pressures. Jobs are rarely as easy as they're depicted—especially if you want to do them right. And finding help is never as easy as it's portrayed—regardless of good intentions. You can usually expect twice as much work as a recruiter promises.

This is not to say that you should automatically reject any job you're offered. But do accept responsibilities with your eyes wide open.

Before responding to a recruiter, ask yourself the following questions:

● **Am I rushing into this?** Always give yourself time to think, pray and examine the issues. Take at least 24 hours. Three or four days is better. A week is best. Mull over this question as you ask the others.

● **Who knows about this job?** Find the person who last held the job. Ask some questions:

1. How much time did it require for meetings? for preparation?

2. What hidden responsibilities go along with the job? For example, does being the chairperson of Committee A automatically make you a member of Task Force B and Council C?

3. What was the biggest frustration you experienced in this job?

4. What was the greatest joy?

5. How many people helped you? Where did they come from? Are they returning next year?

● **What, specifically, are the responsibilities?** Get a clear and complete job description. Often in the church it isn't written, so you'll have to drag it out of someone. Sit down together and go through the year, chronologically. What would I do in January? What would I do in February? And so on.

● **What, realistically, are my own limits?** How much time do I have? How much energy? What are my skills and gifts? How will they help me do this job well?

● **Is it something I want to do?** Do I anticipate any joy in this job? Do I expect to have fun with it? Or am I doing it simply because I think I ought to? Have I done this type of thing before? How did it go?

● **Am I the best person for this job?** Even if I could do the job well, am I the best person to do it? Is there someone else in the church who would do a good job and needs to be doing something like this? Has that person been contacted?

● **Is the timing right?** All things being equal, is everything else in my life going well enough that I can do this job and feel good about it?

● **What are my priorities?** What do I want to accomplish this year? What are my personal goals and my goals for the church? What do I want to see when I look back on this year? Is saying yes to this job going to advance or detract from my priorities?

Remember, the goal is not to say no to everything or yes to everything. The goal is to say yes to the things you choose and no to the rest.

How to Say No

I don't know if it's true, but I once heard that in ancient Japan there was no word for no. There were simply hundreds of ways to say yes, about half of which meant no.

Perhaps that's what we all need: a way to say no that makes the person hearing it feel affirmed but keeps us from doing things we shouldn't do.

We need an affirming way to say no.

I used to say: "I'm sorry. I really am. I'd love to, but I just can't." But it left me feeling empty and negative.

So I found a more positive approach that affirms what I'm already doing: "I'm flattered that you asked. Right now, though, my schedule is full."

The "Positive Nos" chart gives some positive alternatives to some of the common ways we say no. After you've read a few, come up with some of your own.

Of course, these alternatives are designed to make saying no easier for you. They make "no" sound positive and affirming.

You're absolutely free, however, to use the "n" word. All you have to do is smile, thank the person for thinking of you with such an important job, and then open your mouth and say . . . no.

With a little practice, you'll be surprised how easy it gets.

Positive Nos

Negative	Positive
I'm just too busy. I'm buried in stuff right now.	My schedule is full this year. Maybe at some time in the future I'll be able to say yes.
I'm sorry. I can't come on Sunday nights. With my husband's job, that's the only night the family has to be together.	How nice of you to ask, but Sunday night is family night at our house.
I wish I could go on the trip but I just can't afford it.	Our discretionary funds are already budgeted for this year.
I couldn't possibly do it. I have two other meetings that week, and I don't like to be away from home more than two nights a week.	I've already promised that night to my family.
I can't be there. I already have a meeting that night.	Tuesday night is taken. (Or, I'm already committed on Tuesday night.)
I can't. I'm just exhausted from all the meetings I've been to this week.	_____ _____ _____
This new job is killing me. I'm beat. Don't ask me to come to another meeting.	_____ _____ _____
The school, the church, the family, the job—I just can't ask my family to put up with another demand on my time.	_____ _____ _____ _____

When You Say Yes

If, after all these considerations you decide to say yes (which you'll do sometimes), save yourself and those you work with a lot of time and frustration by doing the following:

● **Choose your successor.** From the beginning, train someone to take your place. In about a year this person will be in your place and will probably be calling you to find out the real scoop about this job. If you choose and train your successor, the transition will be quick and efficient.

● **Keep accurate records.** Turn them over to your successor immediately when you leave the leadership position. You'll save many long phone calls, meetings and miscommunications.

● **Evaluate each event or program.** How could it have been done more easily or quickly? Include the evaluation in your records.

● **Don't complain.** How tired we all get of people who accept positions and then complain about them! Do the job as well as you can, then move on. Complainers drive away helpers, leaving more work for themselves.

● **Keep your word.** If you agreed to hold a job for only one year, quit when the year is up—whether or not you have a successor. Staying in the position for a "couple more months" can easily become another yearlong task. Even worse is keeping a job "just until we find someone else to do it." If you're doing it, there's no incentive to find someone else. Often the vacuum left by your resignation is the impetus to find a new leader. If no leader comes forward, maybe the church needs to drop the program. When there's sufficient interest, it will resurrect with new leadership.

■ CHAPTER 8 ■

Time Out

S everal years ago I started working out over my lunch hour. Now that doesn't sound like such a big deal, but you should've heard the grumbling.

First of all, no one had ever heard of a minister having a "lunch hour." People who punch a clock have a lunch hour. But ministers have luncheon meetings. Or they grab a sandwich between meetings or hospital visits. Or they just skip lunch.

Second, it took me away from the church. Okay, if you have to take a lunch hour, take it in your office where you can be constantly interrupted by phone calls and questions. But leave? Go away? Actually be incommunicado for—what—45 whole minutes? Well, it's just unthinkable.

And that's what it was: 45 minutes, three times a week. On the way back to the office, I'd pick up a salad and eat it while I worked on a sermon or Bible study lesson or caught up on my reading.

Finally, people began to get used to the idea. They'd been concerned about my weight, and they liked the newer, leaner look I was beginning to show.

Then one day, about the time I figured everyone had accepted the fact that I was going to work out three times a week, a church member approached me.

"Boy, Dean," he said. "You're looking good. How much weight have you lost?"

"Oh, about 40 pounds," I said. (There was no way he couldn't have known this. I'd told everybody I knew.)

"Well, gee, that's great," he said, nodding his head in approval. "How much more you gonna lose, anyway?"

"Twenty more pounds. That'll put me at my correct weight for my size."

"Good," he said, smiling. "Then you can quit spending all your time at the gym and start being a pastor again."

I wish I'd had the presence of mind to say something witty like "Oh, I'm a pastor at the gym too." But I didn't. I was too hurt and too angry to say anything.

I just smiled and walked away.

□ □ □

You can't wait for other people to give you permission to take time out for yourself. There's always some job that could be done, some chore that could be tended to, some meeting that could be held while you're out taking care of yourself.

When I started doing things more efficiently, I was sometimes tempted to fill the free time I'd created with more tasks. After all, that's what people expect from youth workers. So I'd say to myself: "Gee, it only takes half the usual time to answer mail. Maybe I'll develop a brand-new Bible study for tonight's meeting. That'd be much better than modifying an old one, wouldn't it?"

But adding more tasks to fill your time only adds to the stress and burnout. If you're like most dedicated youth workers, you already do enough. So use the time you've made to take care of yourself and your family.

There are five primary ways to take care of yourself once you've decided to make and take the time:

- Recreation
- Health
- Family and Friends
- Your Spiritual Life
- Days Off

These activities must be the sacred cows of your schedule—inviolable. Unquestionable. Absolute. Let's look at them.

Recreation

Make recreation part of every day. Recreation re-creates you, your energy, your perspective, your commitments. I jog for 20 minutes every morning and write for fun every evening before bed. I start and end each day doing something for myself.

Recreation need not be vigorous activity, though it can be. Whatever it is, it should be an activity you do for you and you alone. This doesn't mean you don't do it *with* others; it means you don't do it *for* them.

Some people jog, and others write poetry. Work in the garden, train the dog, build bird feeders, refinish antique furniture—do whatever you choose! Make it as different from your work as you can.

When you finish, you should feel re-created. If you don't, try something else.

Use the "Recreation Checklist" to help you determine what kind of recreation is right for you.

Health

In itself, taking time out creates better mental and physical health. But we also need to make time to attend specifically to health needs.

● **Exercise**—Recently we've learned that one of the best ways to combat stress is through vigorous physical exercise. If you're not exercising, you're depriving yourself, your family and your ministry of the best you have to offer. Find an exercise you're comfortable with. Start slow. Work up to at least 20 minutes, three times per week.

Here's only a partial list of cheap, easy exercises that can help you feel and work better:

● Walking—briskly, arms pumping or swinging.
● Jogging—one mile in 10 minutes.
● Running—for the serious athlete only.
● Weightlifting—always with a partner.
● Aerobic dancing—with a qualified instructor.
● Swimming—for an excellent workout.

Recreation Checklist

1. List 10 things you really enjoy doing:

1) _____ 6) _____
2) _____ 7) _____
3) _____ 8) _____
4) _____ 9) _____
5) _____ 10) _____

2. Now choose three you enjoy enough to do every day. List them in the first column of the chart below.

3. For each one of these activities, list the following information in the appropriate column:

● What is the minimum amount of time it takes to do this?

● How much does this activity cost per day?

● What do you need (tools, equipment, clothing) to do this regularly?

Activity	Time	Cost	What you'll need
1.			
2.			
3.			

Now choose one of these things to do tomorrow:
Which one do you choose? _____
What time are you going to do it?_____
For how long will you do it each day?_____

● Bicycling—fun for the whole family.

● Nautilus or Universal machine—for a quick, complete workout at a recreation facility.

Check with your doctor if you're not sure where to start or what's appropriate for you.

● **Diet**—Watch what you eat. A balanced diet keeps you and makes you feel good. Fun food is okay occasionally, but don't make it the bulk of your menu.

● **Health care**—Find a doctor and dentist you like and respect. Visit them *regularly*. Make them part of your personal health-care team.

Family and Friends

Youth work is only part of what you do and who you are. Jobs come and go, but family and friends are forever. And nothing overcomes stress like a hug from someone who loves you.

The greatest tragedy I've witnessed in church is the number of committed Christian ministers who've sacrificed their family lives for their ministries. They discover too late in life that they've missed some of the most important gifts God has given them. They have colleagues but no close friends. They have kids but they don't know them. Their spouse is more like a business partner than a lover.

● **Family events**—Write family events on your calendar *in ink*. Don't change them to schedule a church meeting.

Like any other important event, the PTA meetings, scouting events, family reunions, concerts and sports banquets should be part of your schedule. Don't squeeze them between church meetings so family members feel like they're intruding on your schedule. Plan church meetings around these events—not the other way around.

● **Mealtimes**—Schedule at least three meals a week as family meals. (Single people: Eat home-cooked meals with roomates or friends.) Tough, right? Okay, start with one and work up to three. And don't place a double standard on the family. If you expect family times to be important to your kids, make them important to you. Turn off the television and radio. Talk. And don't take phone calls during a meal.

I heard a speaker once who told about having dinner at a friend's house when his friend received a call from the President of the United States. Much to his guest's amazement, the host asked if he could call the President later—he was having dinner with a special friend. That guest felt *important*.

Do you want your family to feel important? Don't take calls during meals. No matter who's calling. If you have an answering machine, let it take messages during meals and other family times. Then call back when it doesn't interfere with family time.

During the meal, intentionally ask questions to get conversation rolling. At first, this method of starting conversations may seem stiff and formal. We tend to be more at home with spontaneity. But spontaneity can be something to hide behind when you don't want to work at your relationships. Table talk can help you be serious, intentional and, at the same time, comfortable with your family relationships. Of course, you'll want to stay away from questions that can be answered with a simple yes or no. There are four basic kinds of questions that work well. Here are some samples. Add some of your own.

1. Objective questions—These are simple, direct questions that recall the day's events: What did you learn today? What did you hear that was worth repeating? What colors, sounds, words or phrases do you remember from the day?

2. Subjective questions—These ask how you feel about your experiences: What did you laugh about today? When did you feel sad, anxious, angry, upset, giddy?

3. Fantasy questions—These are the "what if" questions that children love: What if you were a member of the opposite sex? How would it have made your day different? How would the day have been different if you'd found a $100 bill on the sidewalk this morning?

4. Faith questions—These are questions that bring our Christian faith into our reflections on the day: Where did you see God's hand at work today? Did you see evidence of sin and/or reconciliation today? What did it look like?

After using this method a few times, don't be surprised

if family members start saving up observations and stories so they can share them at the table.

● **Extended family and friends**—Tend to your extended family and friends as well as those immediately around you. Call your mother—for no reason except to talk. Write letters to your friends. Invite someone to dinner. Nothing fancy—hamburgers are great. In short, attend to the relationships in your life.

Your Spiritual Life

When the crunch of unsolved problems, administrative details, retreat plans and program development begins to squeeze you, your personal, devotional life may be the first thing to go.

Don't let it. However you choose to maintain your spiritual growth—Bible studies, prayer, meditation—do it regularly. It's not only important to your ministry; it's important to your own spiritual health.

For me, Bible study is where I find my spiritual sustenance. Here's a quick Bible study method I've used for the past eight years. It's my primary method for writing sermons, but I also use it when I'm not preaching. It keeps me on my toes and keeps me in touch with the scriptures.

It only takes about three hours a week (30 minutes a day, average). It always astonishes me how the passage I'm studying speaks to the week's events.

Here's the method. Try it, refine it for your own purposes and stick to it. It'll provide you with spiritual food for the week—not to mention for sermons, sermonettes and devotions.

● **Monday** (15 minutes)—Choose a scripture passage. Type it out, word for word, in the middle of a clean piece of typing paper. Hang it in a prominent place. I tape it to my desk lamp. Also, I usually use my favorite translation at this stage. (I use other translations later.)

Read the passage a couple of times. Then put it in the back of your mind and let it simmer for 24 hours.

● **Tuesday** (20 minutes)—After the passage simmers for a day, you'll probably have some questions, remarks or observations. Write them on small pieces of paper and tape them to the sheet with the passage.

Now read the passage again, out loud. Use inflection to emphasize different words and different passages as you read. Note and post any new questions or observations. Return the passage to low heat and let it simmer another 24 hours.

● **Wednesday** (30 minutes)—Note and post any new questions and/or observations that have come to mind through the past day. Perhaps the passage has reminded you of some stories or experiences. Note them in a couple of words and post them as well.

Now read the passage again. Go to your Bible and read the context of the verses before and after your chosen passage.

Read your passage in other translations.

Begin asking questions such as: So what? What's the point of this passage?

● **Thursday** (5 minutes)—I just let the passage simmer some more. Keep your eyes open for new stories and observations that relate to the passage.

● **Friday** (1 hour)—Again, note and post your questions, observations and stories on the main sheet.

Get two good commentaries and read what scholars say about this passage. Compare these with your own gut reactions, and note any new observations or insights you have.

Now it's time to get ruthless. Make a decision based on your best observations and insights. Complete this sentence: The main point of this passage is . . .

Take down your passage and the attached pieces of paper. Focus on those thoughts that relate to the main point. Try to answer questions that the commentaries couldn't help answer.

Put your thoughts back on low heat and let them simmer overnight.

● **Saturday** (40 minutes)—While the kids are watching cartoons and Mom is sleeping in, I fix myself a cup of coffee and organize my thinking about my passage.

Using everything I've collected through the week, I create an outline that would bring out the passage's main point.

This outline can become the basis for a sermon. I file this outline with others that relate to the main point. Later I may use it for a devotion, sermon or pep talk. Or I may never use it except for my own spiritual growth.

Either way, I've kept in touch with the scriptures. On Monday I'll begin again.

Days Off

Days off—regular days off, extra days off and vacations—are such a vital and important part of self-care that I'll deal with them in a chapter all their own (Chapter 9).

Weekly Planning

One of the main reasons we never find time for ourselves is that we don't know where all our time goes. One task runs into another, and before we know it, it's midnight.

I've found that using a weekly schedule helps me keep track of my schedule. I use it to plot my week in advance. Then I stand back and look for the balance necessary for my own peace of mind and a productive ministry.

Here are some hints on how to fill out the schedule.

● Get out your pocket calendar and write on the chart all the engagements you've made for this week.

● Fill in the important health and relationship items that need to be on your agenda (family, jogging, doctor appointments).

● Look at the next couple of weeks in your pocket calendar and see what things you need to be working on in advance. Block out work time on your chart.

● Fill in some of the blank spaces with chores or errands you'd like to get done.

● Leave time between activities to shift gears, travel and make other transitions.

● Leave some open blocks to take care of things that come up without warning.

● Be flexible. You may have to change some things.

Now stand back and look at your chart. Does it show a week that moves too quickly toward Sunday? Or does it

Sample Weekly Schedule

	Morning	Afternoon	Evening
Monday JUNE 6	7 - JOB 8 - STAFF MEETING - BREAKFAST WORK ON YOUTH NEWSLETTER	WORK ON SUNDAY SCHOOL LESSON	5:30 SUPPER W/FAMILY 7:30 CHRISTIAN ED. MEETING
Tuesday JUNE 7	7 - JOB PLAN PROGRAM FOR PARENTS NIGHT MAIL NEWSLETTER	STUDY PHONE CALLS - RECRUIT VOLUNTEERS FOR PARENTS NIGHT	PHONE CALLS - RECRUIT VOLUNTEERS FIND BABYSITTER FOR SAT. NITE
Wednesday JUNE 8	7 - MENS PRAYER BREAKFAST 8:30 - MISC. OFFICE WORK	12 N. - ECUMENICAL LUNCH - PASTORS 3 - COUNSELING APPOINTMENT 4 - JOB	5:30 - SUPPER W/FAMILY 7:30 - YOUTH COUNCIL MEETING
Thursday JUNE 9	7 - JOB 7:30 - BREAKFAST W/FAMILY	OFF	
Friday JUNE 10	7 - JOB OFFICE WORK	COMPLETE SUNDAY SCHOOL LESSON	
Saturday JUNE 11	10 - CAR WASH BEGINS	3 - CAR WASH ENDS	6 - DINNER OUT W/JEAN 7:30 - MOVIE
Sunday JUNE 12	9:30 - SR. HI. SUNDAY SCHOOL CLASS 11:00 - WORSHIP 12:30 - BRUNCH W/YOUTH STAFF		6 - SET UP FOR PARENTS NIGHT 7 - PARENTS NIGHT PROGRAM 8:30 - CLEAN UP

Weekly Schedule

	Morning	Afternoon	Evening
Monday			
Tuesday			
Wednesday			
Thursday			
Friday			
Saturday			
Sunday			

move smoothly and efficiently, taking care to get the work done, but taking care of the worker as well? Have you left time for rest and relaxation? Do you have time to talk with your children or youth group members if a crisis arises? Are you going to do any Bible study this week? When?

You don't have to put everything on the chart—only the really important, must-do things. This will help you determine your priorities for the week—and for weeks ahead.

One other note: I like to have a chalkboard in my office. On it I write upcoming items that I need to think about soon:

Junior high retreat   PTA meeting
Senior high dance at school Speech for ladies group
Summer workcamp   Newsletter
Parents night program   Sermon (end of month)
Ben's Pinewood Derby   Bible study lesson

That way I have these things before me. My mind can simmer on them even when I'm not working directly toward them. Some neat ideas and interesting solutions come from letting things simmer.

Also, when I get a lull in my schedule I can look at my chalkboard for something to spend the time on.

More Than Goofing Off

Taking time out may feel like goofing off. You're afraid of what people will say or think if they "catch" you.

So you wait for someone to give you permission. But the permission never (or rarely) comes. Everyone wants a piece of you; everyone wants you to do something.

Ultimately, *you* must decide to do things for yourself. (If you think about it, self-care really isn't just for yourself, is it?) Self-care contributes to your well-being, your life and your ministry. You owe it not only to yourself, but also to your youth group and God.

So this Monday, look your secretary, spouse and/or children straight in the eyes and say the following words, filling in the appropriate blanks:

"_____(Name)_____ , for the next_____
minutes I'm going to be ____(jogging, studying, sleeping,
____thinking, talking on the phone with my mother).
I don't want to be disturbed. Please____(hold my calls,
____take a message, get lost, don't bother me, watch
____television, play outside)____ until I tell you otherwise. Thank you, and goodbye."

Trust me. You'll be glad you did.

CHAPTER 9

Getting Away

I t was summer, and I was about 7 years old. The temperature hovered in the low 100s for more than a week. The farms were drying up.

I remember lying on a big, wooden swing in our back yard with my stomach pressed to the seat, my bare feet dragging lazily back and forth through the powdery dust. Back and forth, back and forth, twist and turn, twist and turn.

Finally I sighed, wriggled off the swing and shuffled toward the house.

The screen door slammed behind me, just missing my heels as I entered the kitchen. My mother wasn't immediately in sight. So I opened by mouth and projected a perfect whine as loudly as I could:

"Mah-ah-ah-ah-ah-m. I'm bo-o-o-o-o-o-o-o-red."

I look back now and wonder what was wrong with me. How could I have been so stupid? Ah, for just one day like that; nothing to do, no decisions to make, no responsibilities. Just swinging back and forth making dust clouds.

Like you, I spend most of my days working 10 to 12 hours planning programs and fund-raisers, making calls to recruit leaders and drivers, writing sermons and Sunday school lessons, solving problems, getting ready for meetings. When I take a day off, I want it to be like one of those lazy, long, hot summer days when I had absolutely nothing to do.

We all need a day like that at least once a week if we're going to do the other six days right. (Even God took the seventh day off!) So here I offer my advice on how to get

and spend the three most important kinds of days off:
- regular days off;
- extra days off; and
- vacations.

How to Get Days Off

Getting a day off isn't always easy. They're not given; they have to be taken. And even when they are given, they're given grudgingly. So before we talk about specific days off, we have to figure out how to get them.

The secret to getting a day off is simple: Announce it boldly and with conviction. A staff meeting is a good time. Or go to whatever committee oversees your job. Whoever you go to and whenever you do it, be bold.

Picture yourself as Mickey Rourke, *The Pope of Greenwich Village*, where he's going to face down the mob boss. Rourke shaves and puts on expensive cologne. He gets his best suit out of the plastic dry-cleaning bag and puts it on. He stops to get his shoes shined. He combs his hair about a thousand times.

Then he marches straight into an old coffee shop and plops right down in front of the mob boss. Everyone— Rourke, the mob boss, the tough guys standing around, the audience in the theater—knows he's in charge.

That image may be a little heavy, but you get the picture. March into that staff meeting. Sit down. Open your notebook. And say: "Before we get started here, I need to make an announcement. From now on, Tuesday is going to be my regular day off."

Now watch for a reaction. Nothing? Good. You're home free. If, on the other hand, people raise authentic problems, have a fall-back position. "Okay, Thursday then." The day is negotiable. The principle is not.

Vacations and extra days off work pretty much the same way. The only difference is that it helps to throw a little pop-psychology in these cases: Use the word "need." People use it all the time—so much, in fact, they are no longer really sure what it means. To them it means something like "want," only stronger.

So use it like this:

● "I'm sorry, I won't be able to be at that meeting. I *need* to be off that day."

● Or: "Excuse me, I hate to change the subject. But I *need* to talk about vacations. You see, I *need* to take my two weeks during the first two weeks of August."

See the difference? If you just said "I want to be off that day," they might think: "You want? You want? Who are you to want?" But if you use the word "need" they'll think: "Oh my gosh! You need! Well, if you need, maybe we'd better do everything we can to see to it."

It works for me.

Now that you've established that you won't work on a given day or group of days, it's time to decide what you *will* do when you're not working.

The RDO (Regular Day Off)

The most important way to refuel your energy and recharge your ministry is by taking an RDO.

Set aside a Regular Day Off every week. Do something totally unrelated to youth ministry. Or better yet, do something not related to ministry at all. This day is yours. Use it to do something for yourself.

There are only two reasons for the church to call you on your RDO:

1. Clear and immediate crisis or emergency; or
2. World War III.

Make sure someone else is on hand to cover for you. Find someone you trust to handle things in your absence. Then forget about it. Relax.

Planning Your RDO

A friend of mine is so serious about his RDO that he plans a schedule for it. Here's a recent schedule from his pocket calendar:

Noon	Get out of bed.
12:05 p.m.	Eat something.
12:15 p.m.	Take nap.

2:00 p.m.	Watch talk show.
3:00 p.m.	Go get ice cream cone.
3:15 p.m.	Take walk while eating ice cream cone.
4:00 p.m.	Sit on porch. Watch cars go by.
6:00 p.m.	Fix hamburger.
6:15 p.m.	Eat hamburger in front of television.
7:00 p.m.	Read detective novel.
11:00 p.m.	Go to bed.

Yes, it's a full day. But he takes his relaxation seriously. He's single. But those of us with families could learn from my friend.

To be honest, my own RDO schedule looks like his. Of course, I greet the kids when they get off the school bus, and I sometimes watch television with them.

What Not to Do on Your RDO

There are some things you definitely should *not* do while on your day off. These include:

● **Work**—(For chores, see EDO.) Don't do anything that even remotely resembles work. If you start, you won't be able to stop. People will expect it of you. This prohibition includes all kinds of work, not just church work. Don't do yardwork, housework, income tax work or pet work. Relax. Empty your schedule and your mind. That's why we call it a day *off*.

● **Intense parenting**—It's tempting to feel guilty about all the parenting you don't get done on the other days of the week and to try to make up for it on your RDO. Forget it! You'll end up being tired and resenting your kids for stealing your day off.

On your RDO it's okay to take your kids along on fun things. But it's not okay to do something you hate just because your kids want to do it. Among these things I include:

● going to the zoo;
● playing "Candy Land";
● singing the "Intsy Weentsy Spider";
● going to a video arcade; and
● eating pizza at one of those places that has big robots that look like they're singing.

Your list might be different.

Among things I like to do with my kids (which I can do on my RDO) are:

- going to a ball game;
- going to the beach;
- fishing; and
- baking cookies.

Again, your list may be different. But it's important to know what's on each of your two lists so you don't mix them up on your RDO.

- **Worrying (and problem-solving)**—Sometimes we use time off to think about problems. But that's not rest; it's work.

This is your day off, remember? Put work problems out of your mind. Scarlet O'Hara had the right idea: "I'll think about that tomorrow." If something's bothering you, write it on a list of "Things to Worry About Tomorrow." Then forget it.

About People Who Think You Shouldn't Take an RDO

Occasionally someone will be offended that you actually take a regular day off. After all, don't you just play with the kids in the church anyway? Other people do church stuff on their day off. Besides, the thing they want you to do isn't really work. It's a party or a picnic or a meeting where you don't really have to do anything. Just be there.

So what's the problem? You'll do it on your day off, right?

Wrong.

If people say those things to you, give your best smile. Put on an innocent look. Shrug. Then say, "It's my day off." No excuses. No apologies. An RDO isn't just a right; it's a necessity for your ministry. If you still have trouble, read Chapter 7 again—"How to Say 'No.' "

The EDO (Extra Day Off)

Occasionally, you'll need an EDO (extra day off). This is a day to do all those chores you can't fit into your regular schedule but are driving you crazy because they're screaming to be done.

I use my EDO for mowing the grass, washing the car, painting the garage door, fixing the leaky bathroom faucet, making large quantities of food to freeze and doing other general maintenance around the house. This is a good time for running to the grocery store, dry cleaners, post office, stationery store, shoe repair shop, barber, license plates office, accountant, dentist, doctor, veterinarian, wallpaper store or pharmacist.

To make your EDO work well there are a few things to remember:

• **You can't do everything.** There will always be some things that still need to be done. Keep your expectations reasonable, and start with clear, achievable goals for the day.

• **Start with a plan.** Plot what needs to be done and how you can efficiently do it. Group errands together. Let the food cook while you do something else. Start with something easy, move to something more difficult and end with something easy again. If something is harder than you thought it would be, be flexible. Either drop it and come back to it on another EDO or drop something else so you can get the hard thing done.

Start with a list and check things off as you finish them. You'll get a sense of accomplishment.

• **Don't overplan.** Leave some time to rest.

• **Enjoy yourself.** Put work problems out of your mind and concentrate on mindlessly ironing shirts or scrubbing white sidewall tires.

Make the day fit you. Learn your own rhythms and energy patterns. If you have a lot of energy in the morning, plan the big tasks for early in the day. If it takes you time to get wound up, start with the small, simple stuff and work up to the big tasks. Be sure you leave time to rest and shift mental and physical gears. Mix up the tasks to avoid boredom.

The same RDO rules about phone calls from the office apply to EDOs. I learned this when I was trying to paint a gable on my house. I had to climb down the ladder three times in the first hour to answer the phone.

When to Take an EDO

EDOs aren't things you choose to take; they *demand* to be taken. After all, most people have two days off every week.

Usually the undone chores let you know all by themselves that they need attention. Dishes are stacked to the ceiling. Grass has grown past your knees. The car is so dirty you can't tell what model it is.

Every person has his or her own crisis point when it comes to undone chores. I have a friend who takes an EDO once a year whether he needs to or not. He's a very efficient person and gets most things done in the course of a regular workweek. I, on the other hand, need an EDO about every two or three weeks.

The "EDO To-Do List" is a format I use for listing tasks for an EDO. When the page is full or the time equals six hours, I take a day off and do the work.

EDO To-Do List

Task	Equipment required and cost	Time needed to complete
1. _____	_____	
_____	_____	_____
2. _____	_____	
_____	_____	
3. _____	_____	
_____	_____	
4. _____	_____	
_____	_____	
5. _____	_____	
_____	_____	
6. _____	_____	_____
_____	_____	

Total time required ....Six hours

Vacations

Nothing refreshes and renews like a good vacation. And nothing messes you up like a bad one. The trick is to consider your own needs as much as your family's.

Good vacations require planning. And planning a vacation can often be a renewing experience in itself.

What Kind of Vacation Should You Take?

What refreshes and renews you? Do you like vigorous activity? Do outdoor sports fill you with excitement or dread? Are you basically a jock or a couch potato? Do you like the outdoors, or do you consider cutting your steak with a dull knife "roughing it"?

These questions will help you determine what kind of vacation to plan. A highly active person may want a week or two of activity—some of it leisurely paced, some of it more frantic. A sedentary person may want to "veg out" on the beach or a cabin porch the whole time.

Bobbi is a friend of mine who spends her whole vacation on a Florida beach reading detective stories, taking naps and eating in restaurants.

Clark, another friend, goes backpacking, rock climbing and rappelling for a week. Then he spends another week fishing in Canada.

Neither can understand how the other keeps from going crazy on vacation.

If money is a problem, do what a pastor I know does. Every once in a while he and his family trade homes for a week or two with a colleague in another city. New cities offer lots of adventures: The television works. You get a kitchen. Someone feeds your dog while you're gone. And the rent is priced right. It's a thought.

A couple words of warning:

● Just because you happen to feel, right now, like sitting on the beach for two weeks doesn't necessarily mean you'll want to do that when vacation time rolls around.

If you're planning a future vacation, take heed of past vacations. What has worked? What hasn't? What usually renews and refreshes? Chances are, it will work again.

● Whatever you do, don't try one of those we'll-just-stay-home-and-do-fun-things-around-here vacations. They never work. Sooner or later people will find out you're home and the phone will start ringing.

How Often Should You Take a Vacation?

I thrived in college because I got a vacation every quarter. I still like to work on that kind of schedule if I can, breaking my two weeks up into several small trips: A week at the beach in the summer. Three days in a state park in the fall. Two days skiing in the winter. Two days in a tourist trap in the spring. Whenever possible, I combine a couple of vacation days with an RDO or holiday to get maximum time off.

On the other hand, Bobbi takes her two weeks all together. Same two weeks every year. She likes the consistency and looks forward to those two weeks all year long.

Here's a fun way to start thinking about how many vacations to take next year. The family can help. (While brainstorming, don't worry about money or anything very practical.)

First, list three things you could do if you took all two weeks of your vacation at once:

1. _____
2. _____
3. _____

Now list three one-week vacations:

1. _____
2. _____
3. _____

Now list three three-day vacations:

1. _____
2. _____
3. _____

Now list three two-day vacations:

1. _____
2. _____
3. _____

Once you have all of your options, mix and match them. A little rest here, a little excitement there. Something for your kids here, something for yourself there. You may even be able to keep everyone happy!

Planning a Vacation

Planning a vacation, talking about it, thinking about it, saving for it, buying the things you need for it and plotting your route on a map will all help extend the vacation into the rest of the year.

Start planning early. Collect brochures. Start a quarter collection to help pay for it.

Once you've filled out the brainstorm section earlier in the chapter, write or call for information. Your local library can help you find out where to write. Don't forget the chamber of commerce where you're going.

Once you have information in hand, use the checklist in the "Vacation Budget" to help plan your vacation. Make enough copies of the checklist so you can calculate a budget for each possible vacation.

● **What about money?** Within reason, decide what vacation you need, and then figure out how to raise the money for it. Here are some ideas for financing your vacation:

● Have a garage sale.

● Skip dessert and save the money.

● Save your pocket change at the end of every day.

● Start a "bad word jar." Every time you slip, it costs you a quarter.

● Start a shirt-ironing service.

● Offer to sell baked goods at a local auction or at your neighbor's garage sale.

● Cut out something you do regularly (going to a movie, eating at a fast-food restaurant, buying morning doughnuts or a new tie) and save the money in a jar.

● **Plan recovery time.** When you plan your vacation schedule, allow time to recover and shift gears when you get home. One time I returned from vacation at 5 p.m. and went to work early the next morning. It was disastrous. I

Vacation Budget

Answer the following questions for each possible vacation:

1. Housing (cost for whole vacation)

Cabin $_____	Bed and breakfast $_____
Condo $_____	RV (rent) $_____
Motel $_____	House (rent) $_____
Hotel $_____	Cottage $_____
Camper hookup	$_____
Other _____	$_____
Other _____	$_____
Total for housing	**$_____**

2. Transportation: Miles round trip _____

Auto at 15 cents per mile $_____
Train $_____
Plane $_____
Other _____ $_____
Total for transportation **$_____**

3. Entertainment and recreation

_____ $_____
_____ $_____
_____ $_____
_____ $_____
Total for entertainment and recreation **$_____**

4. Meals and snacks

#_____ breakfasts at $_____ each = $_____
#_____ lunches at $_____ each = $_____
#_____ dinners at $_____ each = $_____
#_____ snacks at $_____ each = $_____
Total for food costs **$_____**

5. New purchases before the trip
(clothes, toys, suntan oil and so on)
Total for pre-trip purchases **$_____**

6. Total vacation cost (add totals from
items 1 through 5) **$_____**

was tired, grouchy and unrested when I got to the office.

Come home a day early so you can ease back into the real world.

Escape!

Whatever you plan and whatever you do in your timeouts, keep your mind in the present. Learn to enjoy what you're doing without worrying about what's going on back at the church.

Claim the time as your own. Use it. Enjoy it.

You owe it to yourself, your family and your ministry.

CHAPTER 10

Living in Reality

J ohn heard from one of his youth group members that
the school had a three-day weekend teacher conference
coming up in a few weeks. Not one to let any grass grow
under his feet, John called the school, found out when it
was, canceled three meetings scheduled that weekend and
immediately planned a youth ski trip.

What a great opportunity for the kids! What a wonderful time they'd have together—staying in a chalet, skiing,
shopping, having morning and evening devotions. He reserved a chalet that would sleep 20, knowing that some of
his 15 kids would want to bring friends.

He sent out registration forms and waited.

Two registrations came back within two days. Great! He
could see it already—toasted marshmallows, songs by the
fireplace, swooshing through the powder.

Three registrations came the next week. A little slow,
but the $100 registration fee might be a factor. No problem
though. His church was affluent. These kids spent hundreds—
probably thousands on less important stuff every month.
And this wasn't just any retreat. This was a Christian ski trip.

One more registration arrived two days before the trip.

Six registrations. Not even half of the kids. What was
wrong with them? Didn't they know this would be a wonderful, Christian experience? He made some calls.

Sharon had three babysitting jobs that weekend.

Tom had a term paper to write.

Mary and Jeff couldn't afford it, they said.

Bill, Susan, Mark, Pete and Terry were all going on the high school ski club's ski trip that same weekend. It was at a better resort, and it only cost $75.

John was heartbroken. How could they do this to him? Where was their sense of loyalty, of propriety, of commitment to the youth group?

And what about their parents? Why didn't they make their kids go? Couldn't they see how important and beneficial this trip would be?

John canceled the trip (losing the $50 deposit). At the next group meeting, he made sure everyone knew how disappointed he was. At the church board meeting, he lifted up the failed ski trip as a symbol of the sad and sorry state of today's young people. Their priorities are convoluted.

Some of the board members nodded their heads sagely. Others, however, knew better. They knew John had a relatively low reality quotient (R.Q.) where kids were concerned. He operated on a fantasy level.

Fantasy Living

Fantasy living starts with an *expectation*, which is usually phrased as an "ought" or a "should." It's almost always laid on someone else. For example: "Christian teenagers ought to support their youth minister's efforts and show up at all programs in great numbers."

Once we've established our expectation, we do the minimum amount of work required. We spend our time waiting and hoping for someone to come along to fulfill our fantasy. (Send out registration cards and wait for kids to return them with a cash deposit.)

But along comes *reality*. Kids are busy. Sometimes they show up and sometimes they don't. Their parents aren't always supportive. The kids get interested in something else and back out of church commitments. And they forget to say thank you to the hard-working youth leaders.

We're disappointed. We feel rejected. We get angry. We throw some guilt at the kids and their parents. We bully them or hassle them into meeting our expectations.

Finally, in despair, we back off. We burn out. We quit

doing youth ministry. We look for something else that will meet our expectations.

It's a sad and dreary story, but it's not uncommon in the church. Expectations and fantasies are the two worst enemies of any Christian community, including youth groups.

German pastor and theologian Dietrich Bonhoeffer put it this way:

Innumerable times a whole Christian community has broken down because it had sprung from a wish dream. The serious Christian, set down for the first time in a Christian community, is likely to bring with him a very definite idea of what Christian life together should be and to try to realize it. But God's grace speedily shatters such dreams . . . By sheer grace, God will not permit us to live for even a brief period in a dream world (from *Life Together*).

As long as we impose our expectations and fantasies on our youth groups, God will confront us with reality.

Reality Ministry

Janet decided her youth group needed some extended time together to have fun and enjoy each other's company in a family setting. Something less demanding than a work-camp but a little longer and more structured than the usual retreat.

After considering the likes and dislikes of her 12 group members, Janet thought of a ski trip. She took the idea to the youth council, which is made up of parents, counselors and kids. What did they think?

They liked the retreat idea, and they shared her concern for structure and fun. But some had questions about a ski trip. Three group members didn't ski. It would be expensive. A school ski club took two trips every year. Could they do something else?

Monique came up with the idea of a "toboggan retreat." She knew about a nearby state park with great sledding runs. Several kids had toboggans, and almost everyone had sleds.

Mrs. Emory added that the park had heated cabins. And

she and her husband could go along and cook to help keep costs down.

Tom brought out the school calendar and found a weekend during the basketball season with a free Saturday night. The group could go up early Saturday morning, sled all day, stay Saturday night, sled most of the day Sunday and return Sunday afternoon, early enough to finish homework.

Everyone agreed on the price, times, modes of transportation and other details and left the meeting. The next day Janet called the state park and reserved two cabins. No problems. She was calling six months in advance for a mid-winter date.

Six months later 10 group members, three friends, two counselors, two parent-cooks and Janet took their retreat. The weather was a little warmer than they had hoped, but they still got to sled. And the fellowship was wonderful. Toasted marshmallows, singing around the fireplace, morning and evening devotions—the whole bit.

Janet was pleased. Her goal had been realized. She said a brief prayer of thanks as she crawled into her sleeping bag.

Reality ministry has no expectations. It has only goals. While an expectation lays a "should" or "ought" on someone else, a goal is a measurable achievement accepted by the person who sets it. For example, Janet's goal was to hold a youth group retreat so group members could spend an extended period of time together in a family setting.

Janet's goal showed her what to do:

- Plan the retreat.
- Publicize it.
- Recruit adult leaders.
- Recruit the kids and their friends.
- Reserve a location.
- Plan activities.

Thus, instead of doing the minimum amount of work required by the job description, we do whatever work it takes to realize the goal.

When reality steps in, it doesn't smash anybody's hopes and dreams. It simply creates problems (sometimes). Problems block us from our goals. They're not tragedies. We endure tragedies; we solve problems.

When the event takes place, we celebrate if it succeeds. If it falls short of the goal, we ask why and make notes for next time.

Then we move on to the next goal. No despair, no hurt feelings, no anger. Just joy in knowing that we did our best. We trust God to do the rest.

Reality Ministry and Beating Burnout

What, you may ask, does all this have to do with beating burnout?

Simply this: Fantasy ministry is ministry without focus. It waits and watches and hopes. It reacts. It gets frustrated and flustered. Its feelings are hurt, and it pouts when things don't reach some standard. It wastes time.

Reality ministry—with its clear, concrete goals—is focused. It evaluates what must be done and how long it will take to do it. It sets aside necessary time to do what must be done. Without apology, it rejects those things that can't be done. And it embraces what can be done with enthusiasm.

To an outsider, there may not seem to be much difference between fantasy ministry and reality ministry. In both cases, kids show up or don't show up. Some things work, some don't. Some meetings move quickly and smoothly, others drag on forever.

The real difference is not visible in the youth ministry's outward "success." Rather it's felt in how the ministers approach their ministries. Reality ministry gives you a different attitude—an attitude that brings new energy and perspective to your ministry. And the difference is rooted in your "reality quotient."

Measuring Your R.Q. (Reality Quotient)

Now it's time to measure your R.Q. The "Reality Test" on page 139 evaluates how firmly your ministry is planted in reality. Simply check the appropriate answer for each question. There's no time limit.

Reality Test

	Always	Often	Seldom	Never
1. I feel pretty much on top of things that go on in the youth group.	☐	☐	☐	☐
2. I feel my youth group kids don't appreciate the amount of work it takes to do this job well.	☐	☐	☐	☐
3. I'm happy doing youth ministry.	☐	☐	☐	☐
4. I feel exhausted after a youth group meeting.	☐	☐	☐	☐
5. I feel confident about our programs for the young people.	☐	☐	☐	☐
6. I'm behind in my planning.	☐	☐	☐	☐
7. I enjoy my youth group kids.	☐	☐	☐	☐
8. I let the congregation know when things aren't going the way they should in the youth group.	☐	☐	☐	☐
9. When a program fails, I shrug it off and move on to the next thing.	☐	☐	☐	☐
10. The way kids treat each other really upsets me.	☐	☐	☐	☐

Now figure your score:
- Odd-numbered questions: Always, 10 points
  Often, 8 points
  Seldom, 3 points
  Never, 1 point
- Total points from odd-numbered questions _____
- Even-numbered questions: Always, 1 point
  Often, 3 points
  Seldom, 8 points
  Never, 10 points
- Total points from even-numbered questions _____
- Grand total _____

How did you do?

● **If you scored between 50 and 100**—You have a high R.Q. You probably operate in reality mode. You usually have things under control. You rarely worry or complain. You enjoy work and the kids. Your programs usually succeed. But when they don't, you don't dwell on the problems. Instead, you move on. Other people think you have a bottomless supply of energy and ideas.

● **If you scored between 10 and 50**—You may be operating in fantasy mode. You may find yourself worrying a lot. You may come off as a complainer. You probably feel tired, harried and drained much of the time. Your planning is behind. You feel overworked and underappreciated. And you've probably contemplated quitting several times in the past year. You seem to have crises instead of problems, and you aren't sure what to do next.

Creating Reality Ministry

Perhaps you've discovered that you have a low R.Q. Fear not, you can change. Here's how:

● **Recognize the problem.** Examine your anger, frustration, fatigue and disappointment. There's a good chance they result from fantasies and expectations. No doubt you've laid an expectation on someone, and that person didn't come through for you.

● **Turn fantasies into goals.** Do you want to avoid all these bad feelings? Take your expectations and turn them into goals. Here are some suggestions:

Fantasy: Christian teenagers ought to support the church's programs.

Do you hear the heavy "ought"—the big load on someone else?

Try this one:

Goal: To create a program that will interest and attract young people.

See the difference? The goal is a measurable achievement you accept for yourself. Let's do it again:

Fantasy: Administrative meetings shouldn't take more than 90 minutes.

Goal: To run this meeting so the business is accomplished in 90 minutes or less.

And again:

Fantasy: Youth ministers ought to have a day off once a week.

Goal: To take one regular day off each week.

Okay. Now you try it. I'll give you the fantasy, and you write a corresponding goal.

Fantasy: Church members ought to be more considerate of my time when they ask me to do more things than I can do.

Goal: _____

_____ .

Fantasy: Christian teenagers ought to be more attentive and respectful during devotions.

Goal: _____

_____ .

Fantasy: Parents ought to volunteer to help with the spring retreat.

Goal:_____

_____ .

Fantasy: The church ought to pay its youth minister more money.

Goal: _____

_____ .

Are you getting the idea? Keep doing this conversion until it comes to you naturally. Whenever you feel yourself slipping into fantasy ministry, stop and ask yourself: "What expectation is causing this feeling? How can I make the same concern a goal for myself?"

You'll save yourself time and work if you start—from the beginning—with goals. Then you can skip such terrible time-wasters as disappointment, anger, frustration, fatigue, sadness and despair.

A person who operates out of fantasy says "yes" to too much and ends up crying "no!" to everything when it becomes overwhelming.

A person who operates out of reality says "no" to some things. As a result, his or her whole life becomes a great big resounding "yes!"

Letting Go

Several years ago I planned a senior high retreat to Gatlinburg, Tennessee. It was to be a fun time of fellowship, Bible study, hiking in the Smoky Mountains and spending time together.

Before the retreat, Charles' mother called and asked what I thought about him going with us. Charles was a sophomore who was slightly retarded. He'd never attended youth group meetings and he didn't know any of the group members. He wasn't sure he wanted to go. His mother, however, thought this would be a neat thing for him to do.

I had no way of knowing how it would go. But I said it'd be great if Charles wanted to come with us. So he did.

For a while it looked like my worst fears would be realized. When we met at the church, all 12 group members giggled, shouted and laughed as they boarded the church van. Charles was left standing by my luggage-filled station wagon. The van driver invited him to get in the van, but he refused, saying he'd rather ride in my car.

For six hours he rode with my wife and me. He said very little. We pumped him for conversation, but he clearly didn't feel he belonged.

We finally got to Gatlinburg and settled in. Everyone found a room in the house we rented, and I called the group into the living room for orientation.

Charles sat by himself.

For two days, it went like this. Twelve kids laughing, running, enjoying each other and the mountains; Charles hanging with me—cautious, shy and silent.

Finally in desperation I decided to confront the issue. I'd take Laurie and Roger aside. (The group was so small we'd never elected officers, but they were the leaders.) I'd lecture them about reaching out to others and making strangers feel welcome.

My wife wasn't wild about the idea, but I was determined. A good old-fashioned sermon and a little guilt were what they needed.

Then a funny thing happened. We were washing dishes and cleaning up the supper mess. The kids were preparing for free time in town. They'd do the usual stuff: play video games, shop, eat junk food, ogle members of the opposite sex—all the things that make a retreat worthwhile. Charles was drying dishes. I began to panic, thinking Laurie and Roger would get away before I could deliver my homily.

I quickly grabbed a towel to dry my hands when the darnedest thing happened. Just as I turned to locate Laurie and Roger, they were standing beside me. Laurie smiled that heartbreaking smile of hers and said: "Thanks, Dean. Great supper." (It wasn't. Spaghetti and meatballs. Adequate at best.)

Then, with the smoothest, most beautiful motion you ever saw, she took Charles' hand and began leading him toward the door. "Come on, Charles. It's time for you to get out of the kitchen and live a little." And she, Charles and Roger (the strong, silent type) walked toward the door.

As they left, Laurie was talking a mile a minute. Charles was grinning a grin that threatened to crease his face for life. And just before he closed the door behind him, Roger looked at me . . . and winked.

□ □ □

We spend a lot of time worrying about things we can't do. But sometimes we don't have to do them. Sometimes there's another Power that takes care of things for us.

Trust that Power. When it comes right down to it, he's all we have.

Practical Resources for Your Youth Ministry

FAST FORMS FOR YOUTH MINISTRY
Compiled by Lee Sparks

Here's a lifesaver for busy youth workers. **Fast Forms for Youth Ministry** gives you 70 ready-to-copy forms, schedules, checklists and letters to save you time and effort. In just minutes, you'll have ready-to-use documents that took hours to produce and perfect. Each form is designed to help you better organize and manage your ministry. You'll find hundreds of uses for . . .
► Planning checklists
► Evaluation forms
► Sample letters and more
Make your ministry more effective with this practical, useful tool.

ISBN 0-931529-25-5 $11.95

THE YOUTH MINISTRY RESOURCE BOOK
Edited by Eugene C. Roehlkepartain

Stay on top of youth ministry, young people and their world with the most complete, reliable and up-to-date resource book ever!
► Get the facts on today's teenagers
► Find out who's doing what in youth ministry
► Get the scoop on youth ministry salaries
► Discover resources galore!
Depend on **The Youth Ministry Resource Book** to help you plan youth meetings and retreats. Write newsletters. Prepare youth talks and sermons. Work with parents of teenagers and more. You'll find support for your ministry to young people with this handy gold mine of information.

ISBN 0-931529-22-0 $16.95

THE YOUTH WORKER'S PERSONAL MANAGEMENT HANDBOOK
Edited by Lee Sparks

Pick up practical tips, seasoned wisdom and uncommon encouragement. Get page after page of nuts-and-bolts advice from over 30 youth ministry experts to help you . . .
► Relate and keep up to date with kids
► Use volunteers to reduce your workload
► Manage your time and reduce stress
Find out how seasoned veterans manage common youth ministry problems.

ISBN 0-931529-03-4 $16.95